BUILDING A BRAND IN ADULT CONTENT

MIA PHOENIX

Building a Brand in Adult Content: OnlyFans Formula

Cover Artist: Lauren Burch

Published by: Ali the Narrator

Contents

Introduction

Have you ever dreamed of turning your passion and creativity into a thriving online venture? Imagine a platform that not only allows you to showcase your unique content but also provides a direct connection with your fans, empowering you to monetize your talents like never before. Welcome to OnlyFans, a game-changing platform that has revolutionized the way creators engage with their audience and build a sustainable online business.

In a world where the digital realm intertwines seamlessly with our reality, a revolutionary platform has emerged, reshaping the landscape of online creativity and entrepreneurship. This is the story of OnlyFans, a groundbreaking platform that has transcended conventional boundaries, offering creators an unprecedented opportunity to turn their passions into a thriving online presence. As we embark on this journey, we delve into the heart of what makes OnlyFans not just a platform, but a movement, a community, and a beacon of empowerment for creators worldwide.

At its inception, OnlyFans was envisioned as a haven for creativity, a space where artists, educators, fitness gurus, and individuals from a myriad of backgrounds could freely express themselves. It stood as an antidote to the limitations and restrictions often found in traditional media and social networking sites. Here, the power of personal storytelling merges with the potential of direct audience engagement, creating a tapestry of unique, unfiltered, and authentic content.

As we peel back the layers of OnlyFans, we find a platform that is more than just a repository of content; it is a dynamic ecosystem thriving on the principles of inclusivity, empowerment, and creative freedom. Creators from all walks of life find a voice on this platform, sharing their skills, experiences, and passions with a world eager to listen. Whether it's a painter imparting techniques, a fitness expert sharing wellness tips, or a musician serenading a dedicated following, OnlyFans has become a conduit for diverse expressions of creativity.

Central to the ethos of OnlyFans is the concept of a subscription-based model, a feature that has redefined the creator-fan relationship. This model fosters a sense of exclusivity and intimacy, allowing creators to offer personalized content to their subscribers. Fans, in turn, gain access to a world often hidden behind the scenes – a world of in-depth insights, personal anecdotes, and a closer connection with the creators they admire. This symbiotic relationship is the cornerstone of the Only-Fans experience, blurring the lines between creators and their audience, forming communities bonded by shared interests and mutual respect.

Moreover, OnlyFans has emerged as a beacon of financial empowerment for creators. In an era where monetizing creative work often involves navigating through complex and sometimes unrewarding channels, OnlyFans stands out as a straightforward, creator-centric platform. Here, the financial rewards are directly proportional to the creator's engagement with their audience, making it a viable and sustainable model for many. Stories of creators who have transformed their lives through their OnlyFans ventures are not just inspiring; they are testaments to the platform's impact.

But the journey of OnlyFans is not just about the success stories. It's also a narrative of challenges, learning curves, and the evolving nature of digital content creation. The platform's growth reflects the changing dynamics of how we consume media, seek entertainment, and connect with others. It's a story about breaking stereotypes, challenging norms, and redefining what it means to be a creator in the digital age.

As we navigate through the chapters of this book, we'll explore the intricacies of OnlyFans, from its user-friendly interface to the ways it safeguards the interests of its creators and subscribers. We'll hear from a diverse array of creators who have found their niche, built their communities, and transformed their passions into a livelihood. Their stories are not just narratives of success; they are blueprints for aspiring creators, filled with insights, strategies, and the realities of building a personal brand on OnlyFans.

PURPOSE OF THE GUIDE

The purpose of this comprehensive guide is to equip you with the knowledge, strategies, and practical tips you need to embark on a successful journey on OnlyFans. Whether you're a beginner looking to establish your presence or an existing creator seeking to optimize your performance, this guide is your roadmap to unlocking your full potential.

We understand that navigating the world of OnlyFans can be daunting, with its unique dynamics and ever-evolving landscape. That's why we've curated this guide to provide you with a clear and concise resource that covers everything from setting up your account to creating compelling content, building your fanbase, and maximizing your earnings. Our aim is to empower you with the insights and tools you need to thrive on OnlyFans, while also emphasizing the importance of authenticity, consent, and maintaining a safe online presence.

Whether you aspire to generate a sustainable income, express your creativity, or engage with a passionate community, this guide will help you lay a strong foundation for your OnlyFans journey. So, let's dive in and unlock the incredible opportunities that await you on this exciting platform!"

We'll take you on a step-by-step journey through the various aspects of OnlyFans, ensuring you have a solid understanding of how to navigate the platform and optimize your success. Each chapter is carefully crafted to provide you with valuable insights and practical tips that you can implement right away.

Getting Started on OnlyFans

Learn how to set up your account, navigate the interface, and customize your profile to make a strong first impression.

Creating Compelling Content

Discover strategies for producing high-quality and engaging content that resonates with your audience.

BUILDING AND ENGAGING YOUR FANBASE
Explore techniques to grow your fanbase, nurture meaningful connections, and foster a loyal community.

MONETIZATION STRATEGIES
Unlock various monetization methods on OnlyFans and explore creative ways to maximize your earnings.

LEGAL CONSIDERATIONS AND ONLINE SAFETY
Understand the legal aspects and safety measures necessary to protect yourself and your content while using OnlyFans.

Each chapter is designed to provide you with actionable advice, real-world examples, and hands-on exercises that will empower you to make informed decisions and achieve your goals on OnlyFans.
Benefits of Using the Guide

By utilizing this guide, you'll unlock a multitude of benefits that will accelerate your progress and enhance your OnlyFans experience:

Comprehensive Knowledge: Gain a deep understanding of the intricacies of OnlyFans, from account setup to content creation, fanbase building, monetization strategies, and legal considerations.

Practical Tips and Strategies: Discover proven techniques and practical advice that successful creators have implemented to thrive on OnlyFans. Learn how to stand out, engage your audience, and optimize your earnings.

Time and Effort Optimization: Save valuable time and effort by following a structured approach and avoiding common pitfalls. Benefit from the collective wisdom of experienced creators who have navigated the platform successfully.

Empowerment and Confidence: Feel empowered with the knowledge and tools to take control of your OnlyFans journey. Gain the confidence to express yourself authentically and build a community that appreciates your unique offerings.

Personal and Financial Growth: Unlock the potential for personal growth, creative fulfillment, and financial independence through your OnlyFans endeavors. Embrace the opportunity to transform your passions into a sustainable income stream.

By utilizing the resources provided in this guide, you'll be equipped with the necessary skills and insights to maximize your potential on OnlyFans and create a fulfilling and prosperous presence on the platform.

As we embark on this OnlyFans journey together, remember that success is within your reach. Whether you're starting from scratch or seeking to level up your current presence, the key lies in your dedication, creativity, and authenticity. This guide is here to provide you with the roadmap, but it's up to you to take the steps and embrace the opportunities that lie ahead.

Throughout this guide, we encourage you to actively engage with the content, reflect on your unique strengths and passions, and apply the strategies and tips shared. Don't be afraid to experiment, learn from your experiences, and iterate along the way. Remember that building a thriving presence on OnlyFans is a journey, and each step forward brings you closer to realizing your dreams.

So, without further ado, let's dive into the chapters, embrace the challenges, and unlock your potential on OnlyFans. Get ready to captivate your audience, forge meaningful connections, and embark on a fulfilling and lucrative journey that celebrates your passions and individuality. Let's make your OnlyFans experience an extraordinary one!

Getting Started with OnlyFans

Whether you're new to the platform or looking to optimize your presence, this section will guide you through the essential steps and considerations. By the end of this chapter, you'll have a solid foundation to navigate the platform confidently and kick-start your OnlyFans journey.

We'll begin by exploring the benefits of joining OnlyFans, followed by a step-by-step walkthrough of setting up your account. We'll then dive into navigating the platform's interface, ensuring you can effortlessly access its features and functionalities. Finally, we'll discuss the crucial topic of content restrictions and community guidelines, helping you understand what is allowed and how to maintain compliance.

BENEFITS OF JOINING ONLYFANS

By mastering these aspects, you'll be well-equipped to establish your presence on OnlyFans and engage with your audience authentically. Let's get started!

Joining OnlyFans opens up a world of opportunities and advantages for content creators. Whether you're an artist, performer, educator, or influencer, this platform offers unique benefits that can empower you in various ways. Let's explore some of the key advantages of being a part of the vibrant OnlyFans community:

Monetize Your Content: OnlyFans provides a direct avenue to monetize your creative work. By offering exclusive content to your subscribers, you can generate a sustainable income stream. Whether you create photos, videos, tutorials, or other forms of content, OnlyFans enables you to earn directly from your dedicated fanbase.

Creative Freedom and Control: Unlike traditional media platforms, OnlyFans gives you complete creative freedom and control over your content. You can express yourself authentically, explore niche interests, and engage with your audience on your own terms. This level of creative autonomy allows you to build a loyal following based on your unique offerings.

Establish Meaningful Connections: OnlyFans fosters a sense of community and intimacy between creators and their subscribers. By offering a more personal and interactive experience, you can connect with your fans on a deeper level. This connection often leads to stronger relationships, increased engagement, and a dedicated fanbase that supports your work.

Diversify Your Revenue Streams: With OnlyFans, you have the opportunity to diversify your revenue streams beyond traditional methods. By offering subscriptions, selling personalized content or merchandise, and receiving tips from your subscribers, you can create multiple income sources that contribute to your financial stability.

Empowerment and Entrepreneurship: Joining OnlyFans allows you to take control of your own destiny. As an entrepreneur, you have the freedom to set your own prices, create your own schedule, and define your own brand. OnlyFans empowers creators to build their own business and leverage their creativity and passion into a fulfilling career.

Expand Your Reach and Exposure: OnlyFans has a large and growing user base, providing you with an opportunity to reach a wider audience. Through strategic marketing efforts, collaboration with other creators, and leveraging social media platforms, you can expand your reach and increase your exposure, attracting more fans and potential subscribers.

By harnessing these benefits, you can transform your creative passions into a viable and rewarding venture on OnlyFans. The platform offers a supportive and dynamic community that celebrates diversity, creativity, and entrepreneurial spirit.

We'll guide you through the practical steps of setting up your OnlyFans account, navigating the platform's interface, and understanding the content restrictions and community guidelines. Let's move forward and get you started on your OnlyFans journey

SETTING UP YOUR ONLYFANS ACCOUNT

Setting up your OnlyFans account is the crucial first step towards establishing your presence on the platform.

Registration: To begin, visit the OnlyFans website and click on the 'Sign-Up' or 'Get Started' button. You will be prompted to provide your email address, username, and password. Make sure to choose a strong password to secure your account.

Profile Setup: Once registered, it's time to set up your profile. Upload a profile picture that reflects your brand or showcases your personality. Choose an eye-catching display name that resonates with your content and helps you stand out. Craft a compelling bio that gives potential subscribers a glimpse into what they can expect from your OnlyFans account.

Verification and Account Information: OnlyFans requires account verification to ensure the security and authenticity of creators. Follow the verification process, which may involve providing personal identification and additional information. Rest assured that this information is kept confidential and is necessary to comply with legal requirements.

Content Preferences and Subscription Tiers: Determine your content preferences and decide on the type of content you will offer to your subscribers. OnlyFans allows you to set subscription tiers, offering different levels of access and benefits to your fans. Consider what exclusive content or perks you will provide at each tier to incentivize subscriptions.

Payment and Payout Information: Set up your payment and payout information to ensure you can receive earnings from your OnlyFans account. Provide accurate and valid payment details, such as bank account information or alternative payout options offered by OnlyFans. Familiarize yourself with the payout schedule and understand the minimum earnings threshold for withdrawals.

Profile Customization: Take advantage of OnlyFans' profile customization options to enhance your visual appeal. Customize your profile banner, background, and color scheme to align with your branding or personal style. Remember, visual aesthetics play a significant role in attracting potential subscribers.

By following these steps, you'll successfully set up your OnlyFans account and create a compelling profile. Make sure to review the platform's terms of service and community guidelines to ensure compliance with their policies. In the next section, we'll explore the platform's interface and features, enabling you to navigate with ease.

If you have any questions or need further assistance during the account setup process, feel free to consult OnlyFans' official resources or support center. Let's move forward and discover the ins and outs of the OnlyFans platform!

NAVIGATING THE PLATFORM'S INTERFACE

Once you've set up your OnlyFans account, it's time to familiarize yourself with the platform's interface and its various features. Navigating the platform efficiently will enable you to engage with your subscribers and manage your content effectively. Let's explore the key sections and features of the OnlyFans platform:

Homepage: The homepage serves as the central hub of your OnlyFans account. Here, you'll find a feed of your subscribed creators' content, updates from the creators you follow, and recommendations based on your preferences. Familiarize yourself with the layout and explore the content shared by others to gather inspiration.

Messaging System: The messaging system allows you to communicate directly with your subscribers and build personal connections. Respond promptly to messages, answer inquiries, and engage in meaningful conversations. Utilize this feature to create a sense of community and provide personalized attention to your subscribers.

Notifications: Stay up-to-date with the latest activities and interactions on your OnlyFans account through the notifications feature. Notifications will alert you about new subscribers, messages, likes, comments, and other important updates. Regularly check your notifications to stay engaged with your audience and promptly respond to their interactions.

Content Management: Effectively managing your content is vital for maintaining an engaging OnlyFans presence. Use the content management features to upload and organize your photos, videos, and other media. Arrange your content into folders or categories to make it easily accessible for your subscribers. Consider scheduling content releases to maintain a consistent flow and keep your audience engaged.

Subscribers and Subscription Tiers: The platform allows you to manage your subscribers and their subscription tiers. Keep track of your subscriber list, monitor subscription renewals, and analyze subscriber engagement. Regularly assess the performance of your subscription tiers and adjust the benefits and offerings to provide value to your subscribers.

Settings and Preferences: Explore the settings and preferences section to customize your OnlyFans experience. Update your account information, adjust privacy settings, manage notifications, and fine-tune your profile preferences. Take some time to review and optimize these settings to align with your goals and preferences.

By understanding and utilizing these key features of the OnlyFans platform, you'll be able to navigate with ease, engage with your audience effectively, and manage your content efficiently. In the next section, we'll delve into the crucial topic of content restrictions and community guidelines, ensuring you maintain a compliant and thriving OnlyFans presence.

If you have any questions or need further clarification on any of the platform's features, feel free to consult OnlyFans' official resources or support center. Let's continue exploring the vast potential of the OnlyFans platform!

UNDERSTANDING CONTENT RESTRICTIONS & COMMUNITY GUIDELINES

Maintaining compliance with OnlyFans' content restrictions and community guidelines is crucial to ensure a positive and sustainable presence on the platform. In this section, we will provide an overview of the guidelines enforced by OnlyFans, helping you understand what types of content are allowed and what should be avoided. Let's delve into the details:

Respect the Terms of Service: Before creating and uploading content on OnlyFans, familiarize yourself with the platform's Terms of Service. These guidelines outline the acceptable and prohibited behaviors, as well as the legal obligations you must adhere to as a creator. Make sure to review and comply with these terms to avoid any violations.

Explicit Content Guidelines: OnlyFans is primarily known for its adult content, and while explicit content is allowed, there are certain guidelines to follow. Ensure that all explicit content complies with the platform's policies, such as age verification requirements and restrictions on certain types of explicit content. Familiarize yourself with these guidelines to avoid any issues.

Prohibited Content: Certain types of content are strictly prohibited on OnlyFans. This includes but is not limited to child pornography, non-consensual content, bestiality, and illegal activities. It's essential to respect these guidelines and ensure that your content aligns with ethical and legal standards.

Copyright and Intellectual Property: Respect copyright and intellectual property rights when creating and sharing content on OnlyFans. Ensure that you have the necessary rights or permissions to use any copyrighted material and avoid infringing on the intellectual property of others. Only share original content or content for which you have obtained proper authorization.

Community Standards: OnlyFans is committed to fostering a safe and inclusive community. Respect the community standards by engaging in respectful and appropriate interactions with your subscribers and other creators. Avoid harassment, hate speech, or any form of behavior that may harm others or violate community standards.

By understanding and adhering to these content restrictions and community guidelines, you'll maintain a compliant and respectful presence on OnlyFans. Regularly review these guidelines to stay updated with any changes or additions made by the platform.

If you have any questions or need further clarification on any of the content guidelines, feel free to consult OnlyFans' official resources or support center. Let's move forward and explore the art of creating captivating content on OnlyFans!

OPTIMIZING YOUR PROFILE AND BIO

Your OnlyFans profile and bio play a crucial role in attracting potential subscribers and creating a strong connection with your audience. In this section, we'll explore tips and best practices for optimizing your profile and bio to make them appealing and engaging. Let's dive in:

Profile Picture: Choose a high-quality profile picture that represents your brand and captures attention. It should be clear, visually appealing, and relevant to the content you offer. Consider using professional photos or well-designed graphics that reflect your personality and style.

Bio Introduction: Start your bio with a captivating and concise introduction. It should give potential subscribers a clear idea of what to expect from your content and what makes you unique. Highlight your key interests, specialties, or any noteworthy achievements that will pique their interest.

Engaging Description: Craft a compelling description that provides a glimpse into your content and personality. Use concise and persuasive language to describe the benefits of subscribing to your OnlyFans. Consider including any exclusive content, behind-the-scenes insights, or rewards for your subscribers.

Showcase Your Expertise: If you have specific expertise or skills that are relevant to your OnlyFans content, make sure to highlight them in your bio. This can help you establish credibility and attract subscribers who are interested in your unique knowledge or talents.

Call-to-Action: Include a clear call-to-action in your bio to encourage visitors to subscribe to your OnlyFans. Use actionable language and provide an incentive, such as exclusive content or limited-time offers, to entice potential subscribers to take action.

Link to Other Platforms: If you have a presence on other social media platforms or websites, consider including links to them in your bio. This allows interested individuals to explore more of your content and engage with you across different platforms.

Regularly Update Your Bio: Keep your bio up to date and relevant. As your content evolves or you have new offerings, make sure to reflect those updates in your bio. Regularly reviewing and updating your bio shows that you're active and committed to providing value to your subscribers.

Remember, your profile and bio are the first impression potential subscribers have of you and your content. By optimizing them with attention-grabbing elements, showcasing your expertise, and providing a compelling call-to-action, you'll increase the likelihood of attracting and retaining subscribers.

Managing Your Privacy and Security

Ensuring the privacy and security of your OnlyFans account is of utmost importance for both you and your subscribers. In this section, we'll delve into the essential considerations to help you maintain a safe and secure presence on the platform. Let's explore:

Two-Factor Authentication (2FA): Enable Two-Factor Authentication for an extra layer of security. 2FA requires you to enter a verification code sent to your mobile device or email whenever you log in from an unrecognized device. This prevents unauthorized access to your account even if someone gains access to your login credentials.

Content Control and Subscription Tiers: OnlyFans allows you to control the accessibility of your content by offering subscription tiers. You can create multiple tiers with varying levels of content and pricing. Consider offering exclusive content or perks to higher-tier subscribers to incentivize them to stay with you.

Geoblocking: If you prefer to limit your content's visibility to specific regions or countries, you can use geoblocking. This feature allows you to block access to your OnlyFans content from certain geographical locations.

Watermarking: To protect your content from unauthorized distribution or sharing, consider watermarking your media files. Adding a watermark with your username or logo can discourage others from stealing or reposting your content without permission.

Handling Payment Information: OnlyFans handles payment processing for your subscribers, so you don't need to collect payment information directly. However, it's crucial to inform your subscribers about the secure payment process and reassure them that their payment details are handled with care.

Communication Boundaries: Establish clear communication boundaries with your subscribers. While it's essential to engage with your audience, you should maintain a professional distance and avoid sharing personal information that could compromise your privacy.

Blocking and Reporting: If you encounter any inappropriate behavior or harassment from a subscriber, use the platform's blocking and reporting features. This ensures a safe and respectful environment for both you and your subscribers.

Data Protection and Privacy Policies: Familiarize yourself with Only-Fans' data protection and privacy policies. Understand how your data is handled and stored on the platform. Additionally, consider creating a privacy policy for your own account to inform subscribers about how you handle their data.

By implementing these privacy and security measures, you can create a secure environment for both your content and interactions with subscribers. Prioritizing privacy and security builds trust with your audience and contributes to a positive and professional OnlyFans experience.

We'll explore effective strategies for promoting your OnlyFans account to expand your reach and attract potential subscribers. Let's move forward and unlock the potential to grow your fanbase!

Promoting Your OnlyFans Account

Promoting your OnlyFans account is essential for attracting new subscribers and building a strong fanbase. In this section, we'll dive into effective strategies that can help you increase your visibility and grow your OnlyFans presence. Let's get started:

Utilize Social Media: Tap into the power of social media platforms to promote your OnlyFans account. Create dedicated profiles on platforms like Twitter, Instagram, and TikTok to engage with your audience, share teasers of your content, and direct followers to your OnlyFans page. Engage in conversations, collaborate with other creators, and leverage relevant hashtags to expand your reach.

Engage with Your Audience: Build a connection with your audience by actively engaging with them. Respond to comments, messages, and inquiries in a timely and friendly manner. Show appreciation for your subscribers and create a sense of community by initiating conversations, polls, or exclusive interactions.

Cross-Promote with Other Creators: Collaborate with other OnlyFans creators to cross-promote each other's accounts. This can be done through shoutouts, content collaborations, or joint promotions. By leveraging each other's audiences, you can reach new potential subscribers and expand your reach.

Offer Special Promotions: Incentivize new subscribers by offering special promotions or discounts. This could include limited-time discounts, free content previews, or exclusive perks for new subscribers. Promotions can create a sense of urgency and encourage potential subscribers to take action.

Leverage Email Marketing: Collect email addresses from interested individuals and create an email marketing strategy to promote your OnlyFans content. Send regular newsletters with exclusive updates, behind-the-scenes content, and special offers to your email subscribers. Personalize your emails to make them more engaging and relevant to your audience.

Collaborate with Influencers: Identify influencers in your niche or industry who align with your content and audience. Collaborate with them to promote your OnlyFans account through sponsored posts, guest appearances, or affiliate partnerships. Their endorsement can introduce your account to a new and engaged audience.

Create Compelling Content Teasers: Tease your content by sharing snippets or previews on social media platforms or other online communities. This can create curiosity and generate interest among potential subscribers. Use eye-catching visuals, compelling captions, and a call-to-action to direct interested individuals to your OnlyFans page.

Participate in Online Communities: Engage in relevant online communities, forums, or groups where your target audience is active. Share valuable insights, contribute to discussions, and discreetly promote your OnlyFans account when appropriate. Be mindful of each community's rules and guidelines to maintain a positive reputation.

Remember, promoting your OnlyFans account requires consistency, creativity, and active engagement. Experiment with different strategies, track your results, and refine your approach based on what works best for your audience.

In the next section, we'll address common questions and concerns that beginners may have regarding getting started on OnlyFans. Let's continue our journey to provide comprehensive guidance to those venturing into the world of OnlyFans!

FREQUENTLY ASKED QUESTIONS (FAQS):

What is OnlyFans, and how does it work?

OnlyFans is a social media platform that allows creators to share exclusive content with their subscribers in exchange for a monthly subscription fee. Creators can also offer additional paid content, such as personalized messages or tips. The platform provides a space for creators to monetize their content and connect with their fans on a more intimate level.

Is OnlyFans suitable for me? Who can join?

OnlyFans is suitable for a wide range of creators, including artists, models, performers, influencers, and content creators in various niches. The platform is inclusive and welcomes individuals from different backgrounds, genders, and interests. Whether you have a specific talent, knowledge, or unique content to offer, OnlyFans can be a platform for you to connect with your audience and monetize your content.

How much money can I make on OnlyFans?

The amount of money you can make on OnlyFans varies depending on several factors. These factors include the size and engagement of your subscriber base, the quality and uniqueness of your content, your marketing efforts, and your level of dedication. Some creators have been able to generate substantial income from OnlyFans, but it requires consistent effort, high-quality content, and effective promotion to maximize your earning potential.

What type of content can I share on OnlyFans?

OnlyFans allows a wide range of content, including photos, videos, live streams, behind-the-scenes footage, tutorials, and more. However, it is important to adhere to the platform's content guidelines and restrictions. Adult content is permitted on OnlyFans, but explicit content must be appropriately labeled and made available to subscribers who are 18 years or older.

How do I protect my privacy on OnlyFans?

OnlyFans provides several privacy features to help you maintain control over your content and personal information. You can choose to use a stage name instead of your real name, limit access to specific content or subscription tiers, and watermark your content to discourage unauthorized sharing. It's also important to set boundaries with your subscribers and be cautious about sharing personal information.

How can I attract subscribers to my OnlyFans account?

To attract subscribers, utilize social media platforms to promote your OnlyFans account and engage with your target audience. Share teasers of your content, interact with your followers, collaborate with other creators, and offer special promotions or discounts for new subscribers. Consistently provide valuable and engaging content to keep your existing subscribers interested and encourage them to recommend your account to others.

Can I use OnlyFans anonymously?

Yes, you can use OnlyFans anonymously or with a stage name. When creating your account, you have the option to use a display name that is different from your real name. However, keep in mind that there may be legal and tax obligations associated with your earnings, so it's important to consider the legal requirements of your jurisdiction and consult with a professional if needed.

How does OnlyFans handle payments and payouts?

OnlyFans handles payments and payouts through their platform. They offer various payment methods for subscribers to pay their monthly subscription fees, and OnlyFans takes a commission from your earnings. Payouts are typically made on a regular schedule, and you can choose the payment method that suits you best, such as direct deposit or electronic transfer.

What are the best practices for engaging with subscribers?

Engaging with subscribers is crucial for building a loyal fanbase. Respond to comments and messages in a timely and personalized manner. Show appreciation for your subscribers and create a sense of community by initiating conversations, asking for feedback, and offering exclusive content or perks. Remember to set clear boundaries and manage expectations to maintain a healthy and professional relationship with your subscribers.

How can I deal with negativity or harassment on OnlyFans?

Unfortunately, negativity and harassment can occur in any online platform. OnlyFans provides tools to help you handle such situations. You can block and report users who engage in inappropriate behavior or harassment. Additionally, it's important to establish clear communication guidelines and boundaries with your subscribers from the beginning. If you encounter persistent harassment or feel unsafe, don't hesitate to reach out to OnlyFans support for assistance.

KEY TAKEAWAYS

We covered a range of important topics to help you get started on Only-Fans. We discussed the benefits of joining the platform, the step-by-step process of setting up your account, navigating the platform's interface, understanding content restrictions and guidelines, optimizing your profile and bio, managing your privacy and security, promoting your Only-Fans account, and addressing common FAQs.

You now have a solid understanding of the fundamentals of OnlyFans and the tools necessary to succeed. Remember, you have the power to create engaging content, build a loyal fanbase, and monetize your unique skills and talents. Trust in yourself and embrace the opportunities that lie ahead.

It's time to put your newfound knowledge into action. Set specific goals for your OnlyFans journey, whether it's the number of subscribers you want to attract, the type of content you want to create, or the income you aim to generate. Implement the tips and strategies provided in this chapter, and don't hesitate to seek further guidance or assistance along the way. Remember, your success on OnlyFans is within reach if you remain dedicated, creative, and adaptable.

By structuring the conclusion and next steps section in this manner, we leave you with a sense of accomplishment and motivation to move forward. Take a moment to reflect on the valuable insights you've gained, and get ready for an exciting journey ahead.

Finding Your Niche and Target Audience

Welcome to Chapter 3 of our comprehensive guide to OnlyFans. In this chapter, we will explore the vital aspects of finding your niche and target audience on the platform. Understanding your unique selling points, conducting market research, and crafting a compelling brand story are essential steps in attracting the right subscribers and building a successful presence on OnlyFans. Join us as we delve into the process of identifying your strengths, understanding your audience, and selecting the right content categories that align with your brand. Get ready to discover the key strategies that will help you connect with your ideal audience and thrive on OnlyFans.

IDENTIFYING YOUR UNIQUE SELLING POINTS

In the vibrant world of adult content on OnlyFans, it's essential to uncover your unique selling points and strengths that will set you apart from other creators. This section will guide you through the process of discovering what makes your adult content valuable and enticing to potential subscribers. By identifying your distinct attributes, talents, and strengths, you'll be able to create compelling and engaging adult content that captivates your audience.

Embrace Your Authenticity: Authenticity is a powerful magnet for adult content consumers. Embrace your true self and let it shine through your content. What are the qualities and aspects of your personality that make you unique as an adult content creator? Are you sensual, dominant, nurturing, or exceptionally skilled in a particular adult niche? Embrace your authenticity and infuse it into your content to attract subscribers who resonate with your style.

Uncover Your Passions and Interests in the Adult Realm: Reflect on your passions and interests within the realm of adult content. What subjects, kinks, or fantasies ignite your enthusiasm? What aspects of adult content creation genuinely excite you? By tapping into your passions and interests, you'll bring an undeniable energy and enthusiasm to your content that will resonate with your audience. Explore how you can incorporate your passions into your adult content, creating a unique and alluring experience for your subscribers.

Leverage Your Expertise in the Adult Industry: Do you possess specialized knowledge or skills in the adult industry? Are you experienced in a particular fetish, roleplay scenario, or adult performance art? Leverage your expertise to create content that educates, entertains, or fulfills specific desires within your audience. By showcasing your knowledge and expertise, you establish yourself as a trusted authority, attracting subscribers who seek your unique insights and experiences.

Highlight Your Unique Talents and Skills: Identify the talents and skills that make you exceptional as an adult content creator. Are you an exceptional writer of erotic fiction, a skilled visual artist, a talented performer, or an adept dominatrix? Highlight your unique talents and skills in your content, allowing your subscribers to appreciate and indulge in your distinct abilities. Whether it's through seductive storytelling, mesmerizing visual art, captivating performances, or skilled BDSM techniques, your talents will leave a lasting impression on your audience.

Define Your Adult Content Niche: Discovering your adult content niche is paramount to establishing your brand and attracting a dedicated fanbase. What specific genre, fetish, or theme aligns with your interests, passions, and expertise? Define your niche and craft your content around it. Specializing in a particular niche allows you to cater to a specific audience segment seeking precisely what you offer, making you a go-to creator in that area.

Remember, success in the adult content industry on OnlyFans comes from embracing your authenticity, leveraging your passions, expertise, unique talents, and defining your adult content niche. By understanding what sets you apart and incorporating it into your content, you'll captivate and satisfy your target audience.

CONDUCTING MARKET RESEARCH FOR ADULT CONTENT

Conducting market research is crucial for understanding the preferences, interests, and demographics of your potential subscribers. This section will emphasize the significance of market research and provide you with practical tips and resources to conduct effective research, ensuring that your adult content resonates with your target audience.

The Importance of Market Research: Market research helps you gain valuable insights into what your potential subscribers are looking for and what content will capture their attention. By understanding their preferences, desires, and demographic characteristics, you can tailor your adult content to meet their specific needs and create a more engaging and satisfying experience for them.

Analyzing Competitor Profiles: Studying the profiles of successful adult content creators in your niche can provide valuable insights into what resonates with the audience. Examine their content themes, style, engagement strategies, and pricing models. Identify the unique elements that make them successful and consider how you can differentiate yourself while still appealing to the target audience.

Utilizing Social Media Insights: Leverage the power of social media platforms to gather information about your potential subscribers. Analyze the demographics, interests, and engagement patterns of your followers or those within your target audience. Platforms like Instagram, Twitter, and Reddit can provide valuable data and insights that inform your content creation strategy.

Seeking Feedback from Followers: Engage with your followers and create opportunities for feedback. Encourage them to share their preferences, fantasies, and suggestions through comments, direct messages, or surveys. Actively listen to their feedback and use it to refine your content and offerings. Incorporating their desires and preferences into your adult content will foster a stronger connection and increase subscriber satisfaction.

Utilizing Market Research Tools: Explore market research tools and resources that can help you gather data and insights. Platforms like Google Trends, social media analytics tools, and adult industry forums can provide valuable information about current trends, audience interests, and emerging niches. Use these tools to stay informed and make data-driven decisions in your content creation and marketing efforts.

Remember, conducting thorough market research enables you to create adult content that aligns with the desires and interests of your potential subscribers. By understanding their preferences and leveraging market insights, you can position yourself effectively within the adult content industry on OnlyFans.

UNDERSTANDING YOUR TARGET AUDIENCE IN ADULT CONTENT

In order to effectively cater to your target audience on OnlyFans, it is essential to develop a deep understanding of their motivations, desires, and preferences. This section will guide you in gaining valuable insights into your target audience and help you create buyer personas or profiles that represent your ideal subscribers.

Exploring Motivations and Desires: Start by delving into the motivations and desires of your target audience. Consider the reasons why individuals subscribe to adult content creators on OnlyFans. Is it for entertainment, companionship, fantasy fulfillment, or a specific fetish? Understanding their underlying motivations will enable you to tailor your content to meet their needs and provide them with the desired experience.

Identifying Key Demographic Factors: Consider the demographic factors that are relevant to your target audience. This includes age, gender, location, and any other demographic characteristics that may influence their preferences. Analyze data from your existing subscribers, social media followers, or other sources to gain insights into the demographics of your audience. This information will help you create more accurate buyer personas and customize your content accordingly.

Creating Buyer Personas: Developing buyer personas or profiles is a valuable exercise in understanding your target audience on a deeper level. Create fictional representations of your ideal subscribers, including their demographics, interests, preferences, and even their spending habits. These personas serve as a reference point throughout your content creation process, ensuring that you are consistently meeting the needs and expectations of your target audience.

Conducting Surveys and Feedback: Engage with your audience through surveys, polls, or direct communication to gather their feedback and preferences. Ask questions about their content preferences, fetishes, fantasies, and any other relevant aspects. Encourage them to provide honest feedback and suggestions to help you refine your content and improve the subscriber experience.

Monitoring Engagement and Analytics: Regularly monitor the engagement metrics and analytics of your content to gain insights into what resonates with your target audience. Pay attention to the views, likes, comments, and shares your posts receive. Identify patterns and trends in the content that garners higher engagement and use this information to guide your future content creation strategies.

By understanding the motivations, desires, and preferences of your target audience, you can create adult content that captivates and appeals to them. Developing buyer personas and utilizing feedback and analytics will enable you to refine your content strategy and establish a stronger connection with your subscribers.

SELECTING THE RIGHT CONTENT CATEGORIES FOR YOUR BRAND

Choosing the right content categories in the adult industry is crucial for aligning your content with your unique selling points, strengths, and the preferences of your target audience. In this section, we will guide you through the process of selecting the most suitable content categories for your adult content and provide insights on their popularity, potential earnings, and engagement levels.

Understanding Adult Content Categories: Begin by familiarizing yourself with the different adult content categories available on OnlyFans. These categories may include but are not limited to explicit photos, videos, live streams, fetish content, exclusive content, fan interactions, and collaborations. Each category offers unique opportunities for engaging with your subscribers and showcasing your adult content.

Assessing Your Unique Selling Points and Strengths: Evaluate your unique selling points and strengths that make your adult content stand out. Consider the fetishes, niches, or themes that you specialize in and how they can be effectively showcased within the available content categories. This will help you identify the categories that best leverage your strengths and appeal to your target audience.

Analyzing Popularity and Engagement: Research the popularity and engagement levels associated with each adult content category. Look into the success stories of adult content creators within those categories and assess the potential earnings and subscriber engagement they have achieved. This information will give you an idea of the demand and competition within each category.

Aligning with Target Audience Preferences: Keep your target audience's preferences in mind when selecting adult content categories. Consider the interests, desires, and fetishes of your subscribers and how they align with the various categories. Tailoring your adult content to their preferences increases the likelihood of attracting and retaining subscribers who are genuinely interested in your content.

Experimentation and Adaptation: Remember that your adult content strategy is not set in stone. It's important to be open to experimentation and adaptation based on audience feedback and evolving trends. As you gain more experience and insights into your target audience, you may discover new adult content categories or variations that resonate with them.

By selecting the right adult content categories for your brand, you can optimize your adult content creation process and maximize your chances of attracting and retaining subscribers. Remember to regularly assess the performance of your adult content and make adjustments as needed to ensure continued engagement and growth.

CRAFTING YOUR BRAND STORY

Crafting a compelling brand story is crucial in the adult content industry on OnlyFans. Your brand story should captivate and resonate with your target audience, emphasizing authenticity, relatability, and emotional connection. Here's how you can create a captivating brand story for your adult content brand:

Emphasize Your Unique Persona: Start by identifying the unique aspects of your persona as an adult content creator. What makes you different from others? Is there a specific niche or kink you specialize in? Highlight your strengths and expertise that set you apart in the industry.

Showcase Your Authenticity: Authenticity is key in the adult content industry. Be true to yourself and your brand. Share personal experiences, motivations, and passions that make you relatable to your audience. Show them that you are a real person with genuine desires and interests. Connect Emotionally with Your Audience: Adult content is often driven by desire and fantasy. Craft your brand story in a way that taps into the emotions and desires of your target audience. Create a sense of intimacy and connection by sharing stories, fantasies, and experiences that resonate with their desires and fantasies.

Highlight Your Unique Value Proposition: What unique value do you bring to your subscribers? Is it your expertise in a specific fetish or kink? Is it your ability to create immersive role-playing experiences? Identify your unique selling points and highlight them in your brand story. Let your audience know what they can expect from your content and why they should subscribe to you.

Create Consistency in Messaging and Aesthetics: Consistency is crucial for building a strong brand identity. Ensure that your messaging and aesthetics align with your brand story. Use consistent language, tone, and visual elements in your profile, bio, content captions, and interactions with subscribers. This consistency will reinforce your brand identity and help your audience recognize and connect with you.

Engage and Interact with Your Subscribers: Building a loyal fanbase requires active engagement and interaction with your subscribers. Respond to their comments, messages, and requests. Make them feel seen and appreciated. Incorporate elements of your brand story in your interactions, allowing your subscribers to feel connected to you on a personal level.

By crafting a compelling brand story that focuses on your unique persona, authenticity, emotional connection, and value proposition, you can attract and retain loyal subscribers in the
adult content industry on OnlyFans.

REFINING YOUR NICHE AND TARGET AUDIENCE

In the adult content industry on OnlyFans, it is crucial to continuously refine your niche and target audience to stay relevant and meet the changing needs and preferences of subscribers. Here are some key steps to help you refine your niche and target audience effectively:

Analyze Feedback and Metrics: Pay close attention to the feedback you receive from your subscribers. Engage with them through comments, messages, and polls to gather valuable insights. Additionally, monitor your content metrics, such as views, likes, and subscriptions, to understand which types of content resonate the most with your audience. Use this feedback and data to refine your content and focus on the areas that generate the most engagement and positive responses.

Stay Updated on Market Trends: Keep a finger on the pulse of the adult content industry and stay updated on the latest market trends. Explore new fetishes, kinks, and interests that are gaining popularity among subscribers. Stay open-minded and willing to explore different niches or adapt your content to meet emerging trends. By staying informed and adaptable, you can ensure that your content remains fresh and appealing to your target audience.

Explore Collaborations and Partnerships: Consider collaborating with other creators or influencers within your niche or related niches. Collaborations can expose you to new audiences and expand your reach. Look for opportunities to cross-promote each other's content, create joint projects, or participate in themed events. Collaborations not only provide new content ideas but also help you tap into different segments of your target audience.

Reflect on Personal Growth: As you progress in your OnlyFans journey, take time to reflect on your personal growth as a creator. Consider your own evolving interests, desires, and boundaries. Are there new areas you want to explore? Are there aspects of your content that you want to refine or enhance? Aligning your content with your personal growth can lead to a more fulfilling and authentic creative journey, attracting like-minded subscribers who resonate with your journey and evolution.

Adapt and Experiment: Be willing to adapt and experiment with different approaches, content styles, and presentation formats. This flexibility allows you to test new ideas, gauge audience responses, and fine-tune your content strategy. It's okay to step out of your comfort zone and try something new. Embrace experimentation as a means of discovering what works best for you and your target audience.

Remember, refining your niche and target audience is an ongoing process. As you gain experience and insights, your understanding of your audience may evolve. Stay committed to continuous improvement, adaptation, and staying attuned to the changing dynamics of the adult content industry.
Conclusion

Congratulations! You have now completed Chapter 3: Finding Your Niche and Target Audience. Let's recap the key takeaways from this chapter:

Identifying Your Unique Selling Points and Strengths: Discover what sets you apart from other creators on OnlyFans. Embrace your unique attributes, talents, and strengths to differentiate yourself and provide valuable content to your potential subscribers.

Conducting Market Research: Understand the preferences, interests, and demographics of your target audience. Use market research techniques to analyze competitor profiles, utilize social media insights, and seek feedback from your followers to gain valuable insights.

Understanding Your Target Audience: Develop a deep understanding of your target audience's motivations, desires, and preferences. Create buyer personas or profiles that represent your ideal subscribers, considering factors such as age, gender, interests, and spending habits.

Selecting the Right Content Categories for Your Brand: Explore the various content categories available on OnlyFans and choose the ones that align with your unique selling points, strengths, and target audience preferences. Consider the popularity, potential earnings, and engagement levels associated with each category.

Crafting Your Brand Story: Create a compelling brand story that resonates with your target audience. Focus on authenticity, relatability, and emotional connection when communicating your brand story through your profile, bio, content, and interactions with subscribers.

Now, it's time to take action! Apply the knowledge and insights gained from this chapter to attract your ideal subscribers and build a thriving presence on OnlyFans. Embrace your unique qualities, conduct market research, refine your target audience, select the right content categories, and tell your compelling brand story.

Remember, success on OnlyFans is a continuous journey of self-discovery, adaptation, and growth. Stay committed, be consistent with your content, and always listen to your subscribers' feedback.

CREATING COMPELLING CONTENT

We will dive into the exciting world of creating compelling content on OnlyFans. As an aspiring or established content creator, you understand the significance of captivating your audience and standing out from the crowd. This chapter is dedicated to equipping you with the knowledge and strategies to produce high-quality, engaging content that will attract and retain subscribers.

Creating compelling content is a vital aspect of your journey on Only-Fans. It not only showcases your unique personality, talents, and creativity but also establishes a strong connection with your audience. In this chapter, we will explore various aspects of content creation, from brainstorming content ideas to planning your content calendar, producing high-quality photos and videos, and incorporating creativity, variety, and storytelling into your content.

You will discover the power of effective content production, which goes beyond simply sharing explicit material. It is about expressing your individuality, sharing your passions, and providing value to your subscribers. We will explore different techniques, tools, and strategies to help you produce content that captivates, engages, and keeps your audience coming back for more.

By the end of this chapter, you will have a solid understanding of how to create content that reflects your brand, resonates with your target audience, and sets you apart in the competitive landscape of OnlyFans. So, let's dive in and unlock the secrets to creating compelling content that will elevate your presence on OnlyFans and attract a dedicated fan base.

BRAINSTORMING ADULT CONTENT IDEAS

One of the first steps in creating compelling adult content on OnlyFans is to brainstorm ideas that resonate with your niche, target audience, and unique selling points. In this section, we will guide you through the process of generating creative adult content ideas and planning your content calendar for consistent delivery.

To start, take some time to reflect on your personal interests, fantasies, and boundaries. Consider what sets you apart from other adult content creators and how you can showcase your individuality through your content. Brainstorm different themes, fetishes, roleplays, or scenarios that align with your brand and would captivate your adult audience.

Additionally, conduct market research within the adult entertainment industry and stay informed about the latest trends and preferences. Analyze what adult content performs well among your target audience and identify opportunities to put your own unique twist on popular themes. This will help you create adult content that is both authentic to you and appealing to your subscribers.

Once you have a list of adult content ideas, it's important to plan and organize your content calendar. A well-structured content calendar ensures that you consistently provide valuable and enticing adult content to your subscribers. Consider the frequency of your content updates and allocate specific themes or scenarios to different days or weeks.

Take advantage of scheduling tools and apps that can help you streamline your adult content planning process. These tools allow you to plan ahead, schedule posts in advance, and maintain a consistent presence on OnlyFans. Remember, consistency is key in building a loyal fan base and keeping your subscribers engaged.

By brainstorming adult content ideas and planning your content calendar, you set the foundation for a successful journey in creating captivating adult content on OnlyFans. So, grab a notebook, let your creativity flow, and start shaping your adult content strategy to enthrall your audience and establish your unique presence on the platform.

PRODUCING HIGH-QUALITY ADULT CONTENT

In this section, we will explore the essential aspects of producing high-quality adult content that captivates your audience on OnlyFans. We will provide practical tips and techniques to create professional and visually appealing photos, videos, and other media that showcase your unique attributes and entice your subscribers.

Equipment Recommendations: Investing in the right equipment can significantly enhance the quality of your adult content. Consider using a high-resolution camera, quality lenses, and professional lighting equipment to capture clear and visually pleasing shots. We will discuss different equipment options and provide recommendations based on various budgets and preferences.

Lighting: Proper lighting is crucial for creating captivating adult content. Experiment with different lighting setups, such as natural light or artificial lighting, to achieve the desired mood and aesthetics. Learn how to position your lighting sources, use diffusers or reflectors to control light intensity, and create shadows that enhance the overall appeal of your content.

Framing and Composition: Pay attention to the framing and composition of your shots to create visually striking adult content. Use the rule of thirds, leading lines, and symmetry to compose your images and videos in an engaging way. Experiment with different angles, perspectives, and focal points to add depth and visual interest to your content.

Posing and Expressions: Your poses and expressions play a significant role in creating compelling adult content. Experiment with different poses and facial expressions that highlight your unique attributes and convey the desired mood or message. Be confident, authentic, and explore different ways to showcase your sensuality and personality through your poses.

Capturing Engaging Shots: Create adult content that keeps your audience captivated and eager for more. Explore different shot types, such as close-ups, wide angles, and creative compositions, to add variety and intrigue to your content. Consider incorporating storytelling elements into your content to create a narrative that resonates with your audience.

By following these tips and techniques, you can produce high-quality adult photos, videos, and other media that stand out and attract subscribers. Remember to experiment, find your unique style, and continuously improve your skills to create compelling content that sets you apart from others in the adult industry.

INCORPORATING CREATIVITY, VARIETY, AND STORYTELLING INTO YOUR ADULT CONTENT

We will delve into the importance of creativity, variety, and storytelling when creating adult content on OnlyFans. These elements are essential for capturing and retaining the attention of your audience, making your content memorable, and building a loyal fanbase.

Embracing Creativity: Encourage readers to think outside the box and explore their creative potential. Experiment with different ideas, themes, and concepts that align with your brand and resonate with your audience. Push boundaries, take risks, and challenge conventional norms to create unique and visually stunning adult content that stands out in a saturated market.

Adding Variety to Your Content: Avoid monotony by introducing variety into your adult content. Offer a mix of different content types, such as photos, videos, GIFs, audio clips, or written erotica, to cater to diverse preferences. Explore different settings, outfits, props, and scenarios to keep your content fresh and engaging. By providing a variety of experiences, you can cater to the varied desires and interests of your subscribers.

Incorporating Storytelling Techniques: Engage your audience on a deeper level by incorporating storytelling techniques into your adult content. Develop narratives, characters, and scenarios that evoke emotions, spark curiosity, and create a sense of anticipation. Use elements of suspense, surprise, and progression to keep your subscribers invested in your content and eager to see what unfolds next.

Building a Brand Persona: Develop a distinct brand persona that resonates with your target audience. Define your unique personality, style, and voice, and infuse it into your adult content. This consistency will help you build a recognizable and authentic brand that attracts loyal subscribers. Your brand persona should reflect your values, interests, and the fantasy you aim to fulfill for your audience.

Engaging with Your Audience: Encourage interaction and engagement with your subscribers. Respond to comments, messages, and requests from your audience, and consider incorporating their feedback and suggestions into your content. This level of engagement fosters a sense of community and makes your subscribers feel valued and connected to you.

By incorporating creativity, variety, and storytelling into your adult content, you can create an immersive and engaging experience for your audience. Remember to be authentic, stay true to your brand, and continuously explore new ways to captivate and satisfy your subscribers' desires.

EDITING AND POST-PRODUCTION TECHNIQUES FOR ADULT CONTENT

In this section, we will explore the significance of editing and post-production in elevating the quality and appeal of your adult content on

OnlyFans. While capturing high-quality media is crucial, the editing process can further enhance the visual aesthetics and overall impact of your content. Let's delve into some valuable tips and techniques for editing photos, videos, and other media to achieve a polished and professional look.

Choosing the Right Editing Software: Introduce readers to popular editing software options suitable for adult content, such as Adobe Photoshop, Lightroom, Premiere Pro, or other specialized adult content editing software. Highlight the key features, benefits, and user-friendly interfaces of these tools to assist creators in selecting the most suitable option for their editing needs.

Enhancing Visual Appeal: Provide guidance on enhancing the visual aspects of your adult content through editing techniques. This includes adjusting brightness, contrast, saturation, and color balance to create a visually appealing and consistent aesthetic. Experiment with filters, effects, and overlays to add a touch of creativity while maintaining the integrity of the original content.

Retouching and Perfecting: Explore techniques for retouching adult content to achieve a professional and polished appearance. This may involve smoothing skin, removing imperfections, adjusting body proportions, or enhancing specific features. Emphasize the importance of striking a balance between retouching and maintaining a natural and realistic look.

Video Editing and Transitions: Guide creators in editing their adult videos to enhance the storytelling and engagement. Teach them how to trim, crop, and merge video clips, as well as how to add transitions, text overlays, and audio enhancements. Encourage the use of appropriate transitions and effects to create a smooth and seamless viewing experience.

Sound Editing and Mixing: Discuss the significance of sound editing and mixing for adult content, especially for videos or audio clips. Provide tips for improving audio quality, reducing background noise, and adjusting audio levels. Explore the use of royalty-free music, voice-overs, or sound effects to enhance the overall sensory experience.

Outsourcing Editing Services: Mention the option of outsourcing editing services to professionals or freelancers, such as those available on platforms like Fiverr. Emphasize the importance of finding reputable and trustworthy editors who understand the specific requirements and sensitivities of adult content.

By mastering editing and post-production techniques, you can significantly enhance the overall quality and visual appeal of your adult content. Remember to maintain consistency with your brand image and desired aesthetic while experimenting with different editing styles to find what resonates with your target audience.

ENGAGING WITH YOUR AUDIENCE THROUGH INTERACTIVE CONTENT FOR ADULT CREATORS

We will explore the power of interactive content and its ability to foster engagement and connection with your adult audience on OnlyFans. Interactive content goes beyond static photos and videos, allowing you to create a dynamic and immersive experience that captivates your subscribers. Let's delve into some effective strategies for engaging with your audience through interactive content.

Live Streaming: Highlight the benefits of live streaming as a way to connect with your audience in real-time. Discuss how live streaming can be used to host Q&A sessions, share behind-the-scenes glimpses, provide exclusive content previews, or simply have interactive conversations with your subscribers. Encourage creators to set a regular live streaming schedule to build anticipation and consistency.

Interactive Polls and Surveys: Encourage creators to leverage interactive polls and surveys to involve their audience in decision-making processes. This can include asking subscribers about their content preferences, soliciting feedback on potential ideas, or allowing them to vote on specific topics or themes for upcoming content. Utilize the polling feature available on OnlyFans or external polling platforms to collect and analyze valuable data.

Q&A Sessions and AMA (Ask Me Anything): Foster a sense of community and connection by hosting Q&A sessions or AMAs. Encourage subscribers to ask questions, seek advice, or share their thoughts on specific topics related to your content or industry. Engage with their questions and provide thoughtful and authentic responses, making them feel valued and appreciated.

Collaborations and Guest Features: Explore the potential for collaborations and guest features with other creators or industry professionals. This can involve creating joint content, featuring each other on your respective platforms, or even hosting collaborative live events. Collaborations not only expose you to a wider audience but also bring fresh perspectives and creative ideas to your content.

Exclusive Contests and Giveaways: Engage your audience by organizing exclusive contests, giveaways, or challenges. Encourage participation and offer rewards such as access to exclusive content, personalized shoutouts, or special interactions. This not only incentivizes engagement but also creates a sense of excitement and anticipation among your subscribers.

Community Engagement: Stress the importance of actively engaging with your audience by responding to comments, messages, and direct requests. Make an effort to create a supportive and inclusive community where subscribers feel heard, respected, and appreciated. Regularly acknowledge and reward active subscribers to foster loyalty and encourage ongoing engagement.

By incorporating interactive elements into your content strategy, you can create a more immersive and engaging experience for your adult audience on OnlyFans. Encourage genuine interactions, listen to your subscribers' feedback, and adapt your content based on their preferences to foster a strong and loyal fan base.

MANAGING SUBSCRIPTIONS AND OFFERING EXCLUSIVE ADULT CONTENT

We will explore effective strategies for managing subscriptions and offering exclusive adult content to your subscribers on OnlyFans. Managing your subscriptions well and providing enticing exclusive adult content is key to attracting and retaining loyal subscribers. Let's delve into some practical tips for managing your subscriptions and offering exclusive adult content.

Tiered Subscription Models: Discuss the benefits of implementing tiered subscription models that offer different levels of access and perks to subscribers. Encourage creators to create multiple subscription tiers based on the value and exclusivity of the adult content they provide. Each tier can offer increasing benefits and rewards, such as access to explicit photos and videos, personalized adult messages, or special discounts on adult merchandise.

Creating Special Perks and Rewards: Encourage creators to think creatively about the adult perks and rewards they can offer to their subscribers. This can include personalized adult shoutouts, custom adult content requests, early access to new adult content, or exclusive behind-the-scenes adult footage. The key is to make subscribers feel valued and appreciated for their support, providing them with unique adult experiences and content that they can't find elsewhere.

Balancing Free and Paid Adult Content: Discuss the importance of striking a balance between free and paid adult content. While it's important to offer some free adult content to attract potential subscribers and showcase your adult content style, it's equally crucial to provide exclusive adult content for paid subscribers. Emphasize the value and benefits of becoming a paid subscriber, and make sure that the exclusive adult content justifies the subscription fee.

Regular Adult Content Updates: Encourage creators to maintain a regular adult content update schedule to keep subscribers engaged and interested. Consistency is key in building a loyal adult fan base. Discuss the importance of planning and organizing your adult content in advance, so you can consistently deliver fresh and exciting adult content to your subscribers.

Communication and Feedback: Stress the importance of maintaining open lines of communication with your adult subscribers. Encourage them to provide feedback, suggestions, and adult content requests. Actively engage with their comments and messages, showing that you value their input. Use this feedback to shape your future adult content and improve the subscriber experience.

Exclusive Behind-the-Scenes Adult Content: Offer a glimpse into your adult creative process and behind-the-scenes moments through exclusive adult content. Share sneak peeks, bloopers, or insights into your adult content creation journey. This helps create a sense of exclusivity and connection with your adult subscribers, making them feel like they are part of your adult creative journey.

By effectively managing your subscriptions and offering exclusive adult content, you can provide a rewarding and engaging experience for your adult subscribers on OnlyFans. Encourage ongoing communication, listen to your subscribers' feedback, and consistently deliver high-quality adult content to maintain their loyalty and support.
Conclusion

In conclusion, this chapter has explored the essential elements of creating compelling content on OnlyFans, with a primary focus on adult content. Let's recap the key takeaways:

Brainstorming Content Ideas and Planning Your Content Calendar: Generating creative content ideas and organizing them into a content calendar helps maintain consistency and engagement with your subscribers.

Producing High-Quality Photos, Videos, and Other Media: Investing in equipment, understanding lighting techniques, and mastering composition contribute to producing visually appealing adult content.

Incorporating Creativity, Variety, and Storytelling into Your Content: Keeping your adult content fresh and engaging by experimenting with themes, concepts, and storytelling techniques is essential to captivate your audience.

Editing and Post-Production Techniques: Enhancing the overall quality and appeal of your adult content through editing techniques contributes to a polished and professional look.

Engaging with Your Audience through Interactive Content: Utilizing interactive content, such as live streaming, polls, and collaborations, creates a dynamic and interactive experience for your adult subscribers.

Managing Subscriptions and Offering Exclusive Adult Content: Implementing tiered subscription models, creating special perks and rewards, and balancing free and paid adult content contribute to maintaining subscriber loyalty and satisfaction.

By applying the knowledge and techniques you've gained in this chapter, you are well on your way to creating compelling adult content and building a thriving presence on OnlyFans. Stay focused, be creative, and keep providing unique experiences for your adult audience.

Building & Engaging Your FanBase

Welcome to Chapter 5 of our guide on OnlyFans, where we delve into the essential topic of building and engaging your fanbase. As a creator on OnlyFans, your fanbase plays a pivotal role in your success and earnings. It's not just about the number of subscribers you have, but also about cultivating a loyal and engaged community that supports and appreciates your content.

Building a fanbase goes beyond simply attracting subscribers; it involves establishing meaningful connections with your audience, creating a sense of belonging, and consistently providing value. The stronger your fanbase, the greater the potential for long-term success and financial stability on the platform.

In this chapter, we will explore strategies and techniques to help you attract and retain subscribers, leverage the power of social media platforms to promote your OnlyFans account, and cultivate personal connections and engagement with your fans. We will also discuss effective methods for managing subscriptions, offering exclusive content, and exploring collaboration opportunities with other creators.

Remember, building and engaging your fanbase is an ongoing process that requires dedication, creativity, and a genuine passion for what you do. By implementing the strategies discussed in this chapter, you can increase your visibility, deepen your connection with your fans, and ultimately enhance your overall success on OnlyFans.

So, let's dive in and discover the key elements and techniques to build a thriving fanbase that supports your journey as an OnlyFans creator. Together, we will explore the strategies that will take your presence on the platform to new heights.

STRATEGIES FOR ATTRACTING AND RETAINING SUBSCRIBERS

To build a thriving fanbase on OnlyFans, it's essential to attract new subscribers while also retaining the ones you already have. In this section, we'll explore effective strategies that will help you achieve both goals.

Offer Exclusive Content: One of the key reasons subscribers join OnlyFans is to access exclusive content they can't find elsewhere. Consider offering exclusive photos, videos, behind-the-scenes footage, or intimate live streams that provide a unique and personalized experience for your subscribers. This creates a sense of value and exclusivity, incentivizing them to stay subscribed and even refer others.

Personalize the Experience: Take the time to understand your subscribers' preferences and interests. Engage with them through direct messages, comments, and personalized shoutouts. Tailor your content to their desires and make them feel seen and appreciated. By building a personal connection, you increase the chances of long-term subscriber loyalty.

Incentivize Subscriptions: Encourage potential subscribers to join by offering special incentives or discounts. This could include limited-time promotions, bundled content packages, or early access to upcoming releases. By providing extra value upfront, you attract new subscribers and demonstrate the benefits of being a part of your fanbase.

Consistency is Key: Regularly update your content and engage with your subscribers. Maintain a consistent schedule so that your fans know when to expect new content from you. Consistency builds trust, establishes expectations, and keeps subscribers interested and engaged. Aim for a balance between providing fresh content and maintaining quality to ensure a loyal and satisfied fanbase.

Leverage Social Media: Utilize various social media platforms to promote your OnlyFans account and attract potential subscribers. Share teasers, previews, and snippets of your content to pique their interest. Engage with your followers, collaborate with other creators, and leverage hashtags to expand your reach and visibility. Direct your social media audience to your OnlyFans page, making it easy for them to transition from followers to paying subscribers.

Remember, building and retaining a fanbase takes time and effort. Focus on providing value, personalization, and a unique experience to your subscribers. By implementing these strategies, you'll increase your chances of attracting and retaining a loyal and dedicated fanbase on OnlyFans.

PROMOTE YOUR ONLYFANS ACCOUNT

Social media platforms play a crucial role in expanding your reach, attracting new subscribers, and promoting your OnlyFans account. By effectively leveraging platforms like Twitter, Instagram, and TikTok, you can tap into a wider audience and drive traffic to your profile. Here are some tips and strategies to make the most of social media for promoting your OnlyFans:

Identify Your Target Audience: Understand who your target audience is and which social media platforms they are most active on. This will help you focus your efforts on the platforms that are most likely to yield results. For example, if your content appeals to a younger audience, TikTok might be a great platform to engage with potential subscribers.

Optimize Your Profiles: Ensure that your social media profiles accurately reflect your OnlyFans brand. Use compelling profile bios, consistent branding elements, and a link to your OnlyFans profile in your bio or website section. Make it clear to your followers that you have exclusive content on OnlyFans and entice them to check it out.

Share Teasers and Previews: Generate curiosity and interest by sharing enticing teasers and previews of your content. Use eye-catching visuals, intriguing captions, and snippets that leave your audience wanting more. Create a sense of exclusivity and make it clear that they can access the full content on your OnlyFans account.

Engage with Your Audience: Actively engage with your social media followers by responding to comments, direct messages, and mentions. Foster a sense of community and connection, as this can encourage followers to become paying subscribers. Show appreciation for their support and make them feel valued.

Collaborate with Other Creators: Collaborating with other creators in your niche can help you tap into their audience and vice versa. Consider cross-promoting each other's content, doing joint live streams, or featuring each other in your posts. This mutually beneficial collaboration can expand your reach and attract new subscribers.

Utilize Hashtags and Trending Topics: Research popular hashtags and trending topics related to your niche and incorporate them into your social media posts. This can increase the visibility of your content and attract users who are actively searching for similar content. However, ensure that the hashtags and topics you use are relevant and align with your brand.

Offer Exclusive Social Media Content: Reward your social media followers by occasionally sharing exclusive content or special promotions on your platforms. This not only keeps your existing followers engaged but also entices new users to follow and engage with you. Make it clear that by following you on social media, they gain access to additional content and perks.

Remember to adhere to the guidelines and policies of each social media platform. Avoid direct explicit content on these platforms, but rather focus on promoting your OnlyFans account as a platform for accessing adult content.

CULTIVATING PERSONAL CONNECTIONS

Building personal connections and fostering engagement with your fans is crucial for long-term success on OnlyFans. By actively communicating with your subscribers, responding to messages and comments, hosting live streams or Q&A sessions, and creating a sense of community, you can strengthen your relationship with your fans and increase their loyalty. Here are some tips to help you cultivate personal connections and engagement with your fans:

Active Communication: Regularly interact with your fans by responding to their messages, comments, and requests. Show genuine interest in their feedback, questions, and suggestions. By actively engaging with your fans, you make them feel valued and appreciated.

Prompt Responses: Aim to respond to messages and comments in a timely manner. This demonstrates your dedication to providing excellent customer service and builds trust with your fans. Even if you receive a large volume of messages, prioritize responding to as many as possible.

Live Streams and Q&A Sessions: Host live streams or Q&A sessions on OnlyFans to directly interact with your fans in real-time. This creates a unique opportunity for them to ask questions, share their thoughts, and get to know you better. Consider dedicating specific time slots for these sessions to make them regular and anticipated events.

Exclusive Content for Subscribers: Provide exclusive content that is specifically tailored to your subscribers. This can include behind-the-scenes footage, personalized shoutouts, sneak peeks, or special discounts. By offering exclusive perks, you make your subscribers feel special and appreciated.

Create a Sense of Community: Foster a sense of community among your subscribers by encouraging interactions between them. This can be done through group chats, community forums, or interactive posts where subscribers can share their thoughts and connect with each other. Building a supportive community not only enhances engagement but also encourages fans to stay subscribed.

Offer Special Events or Contests: Organize special events or contests exclusively for your subscribers. This can range from fan appreciation events to photo contests or exclusive giveaways. These activities not only increase engagement but also create excitement and anticipation among your fans.

Show Your Authenticity: Share aspects of your personal life, interests, and experiences with your fans. Authenticity helps create a stronger connection and makes you more relatable. However, remember to maintain appropriate boundaries and share only what you are comfortable with.

Regular Updates: Consistently provide fresh content and updates to keep your subscribers engaged. This can be achieved through regular posting schedules, themed content days, or monthly updates about upcoming projects. By staying active and consistent, you give your fans a reason to stay subscribed.

Remember, building personal connections and engagement takes time and effort. Be patient and genuine in your interactions with your fans. By nurturing these connections, you can foster a loyal fanbase that supports and promotes your OnlyFans account.

MANAGING SUBSCRIPTIONS

Managing your subscriptions and offering exclusive content is essential for creating value for your fans and maximizing your earnings on Only-Fans. By implementing effective strategies, you can provide a rewarding experience for your subscribers and keep them engaged. Here are some tips on managing your subscriptions and offering exclusive content:

Tiered Subscription Models: Consider implementing tiered subscription models to cater to different fan preferences and budgets. Offer multiple subscription tiers with varying levels of access and benefits. This allows fans to choose the tier that best suits their needs and encourages them to upgrade for additional perks.

Exclusive Perks and Rewards: Provide exclusive perks and rewards to incentivize subscriptions and retain loyal fans. These can include access to premium content, personalized messages, early access to new releases, discounts on merchandise or custom requests, or even one-on-one interactions. Make sure to clearly communicate the unique benefits of each subscription tier.

Balancing Free and Paid Content: Strike a balance between free and paid content to maintain interest and encourage conversions. While offering free content can attract potential subscribers and provide a preview of your content, it's essential to reserve your best and most exclusive content for paid subscribers. Find a balance that allows you to showcase your talents while providing enough value to entice fans to subscribe.

Consistency in Content Delivery: Develop a consistent schedule for delivering content to your subscribers. This helps build anticipation and ensures that your fans know when to expect new content. Whether you choose to release content daily, weekly, or on specific days, consistency is key to keeping your subscribers engaged and satisfied.

Listen to Subscriber Feedback: Pay attention to feedback and requests from your subscribers. Consider implementing their suggestions or creating content based on their interests. By demonstrating that you value their input, you strengthen your relationship with your fans and increase the likelihood of retaining them.

Test and Evaluate Content Performance: Continuously assess the performance of your content to determine what resonates best with your subscribers. Use analytics tools provided by OnlyFans to track engagement, views, and interactions. This data can help you identify the type of content that generates the most interest and adjust your content strategy accordingly.

Monitor Subscription Churn: Keep an eye on your subscription churn rate, which refers to the rate at which subscribers cancel their subscriptions. If you notice a high churn rate, assess the reasons behind it and take necessary steps to address any issues. This could involve improving the value proposition of your subscription tiers or enhancing the quality and frequency of your content.

Remember, maintaining a strong subscriber base requires ongoing effort and attention. Regularly evaluate your subscription offerings and exclusive content to ensure they align with your fans' interests and expectations. By providing a rewarding experience and exclusive benefits, you increase the likelihood of retaining subscribers and attracting new ones.

COLLABORATION AND CROSS-PROMOTION

Collaboration and cross-promotion with other creators on OnlyFans can be a powerful strategy for growing your fanbase and increasing your visibility within the adult content community. By partnering with like-minded creators, you can tap into new audiences, attract new subscribers, and create mutually beneficial opportunities. Here are some key points to consider when it comes to collaboration and cross-promotion:

Finding Compatible Creators: Look for creators whose content aligns with yours and who share a similar target audience. Seek out creators with a complementary style or niche that can enhance your content or provide a fresh perspective. Collaborating with others who create content in related genres or themes can help you tap into their fanbase and vice versa.

Building Relationships: Reach out to potential collaborators and establish a connection before proposing a collaboration. Engage with their content, leave thoughtful comments, and interact with them on social media platforms. Building genuine relationships with other creators creates a foundation of trust and makes collaborations more likely to succeed.

Exploring Collaborative Content: Consider various ways to collaborate on content. This can include joint photo or video shoots, creating content together on a shared theme, or even hosting events or promotions together. Collaborative content allows you to combine your unique talents and styles, providing a fresh and exciting experience for your fans.

Cross-Promotion: Utilize cross-promotion to introduce your subscribers to other creators and vice versa. This can involve featuring each other's profiles, promoting each other's content, or even offering special joint subscription bundles or discounts. By cross-promoting, you tap into each other's fanbase and increase the chances of attracting new subscribers.

Maintaining Professionalism: When collaborating with other creators, it's essential to maintain professionalism and clear communication. Clearly outline expectations, establish boundaries, and ensure that all parties involved are comfortable with the collaboration. Respect each other's boundaries and maintain a professional working relationship throughout the collaboration.

Evaluating Collaborative Success: Assess the success of your collaborations by tracking metrics such as new subscribers gained, engagement levels, and fan feedback. Analyze the impact of the collaboration on your OnlyFans account and consider whether future collaborations with the same or different creators would be beneficial.

Collaboration and cross-promotion can significantly expand your reach and introduce your content to new audiences. By partnering with other creators, you tap into their fanbase while providing added value to your own subscribers. Remember, the key to successful collaborations is finding compatibility, maintaining professionalism, and creating content that resonates with both fan bases.

CONCLUSION

We have explored the strategies for building and engaging your fanbase on OnlyFans, with a primary focus on adult content. By implementing these strategies, you can attract new subscribers, retain existing ones, and create a thriving community of fans. Here are the key takeaways:

Attracting and Retaining Subscribers: Offer exclusive content, personalized experiences, and incentives to attract new subscribers and keep them engaged. Continuously provide value to your fans and make them feel special as part of your community.

Leveraging Social Media: Utilize social media platforms such as Twitter, Instagram, and TikTok to promote your OnlyFans account and reach a wider audience. Engage with your followers, share teasers, and direct them to your profile to convert them into subscribers.

Cultivating Personal Connections: Actively communicate with your fans, respond to messages and comments, and create a sense of community. Host live streams, Q&A sessions, and other interactive events to foster engagement and build personal connections with your subscribers.

Managing Subscriptions and Exclusive Content: Effectively manage your subscription tiers, offering different perks and rewards to each tier. Strike a balance between free and paid content to entice subscribers to upgrade while still providing value to those on lower tiers.

Collaboration and Cross-Promotion: Explore collaborations with other creators on OnlyFans who share a similar target audience. Cross-promote each other's profiles and content to expand your reach and attract new subscribers.

By implementing these strategies and consistently engaging with your fans, you can create a loyal and dedicated fanbase that supports your content and helps you thrive on OnlyFans. Remember to monitor your progress, analyze your metrics, and adapt your strategies as needed to stay relevant and successful.

Getting Started with Only-Fans

Welcome to Chapter 6 of our guide to maximizing your success on OnlyFans. In this chapter, we will delve into the crucial aspects of monetization methods and pricing strategies. As a content creator, understanding how to effectively monetize your content and determine the right pricing for your offerings is essential for generating revenue and building a sustainable income stream.

Throughout this chapter, we will explore various strategies and techniques that will empower you to make informed decisions about your pricing structure and discover additional revenue streams beyond subscription fees. We will also discuss collaborations, cross-promotion opportunities, sponsorships, and affiliate marketing as means to expand your earning potential on OnlyFans.

By the end of this chapter, you will have gained valuable insights into setting subscription prices and tiers, exploring additional revenue streams, and leveraging collaborations with other creators. You will be equipped with the knowledge and tools to make informed decisions that align with your brand, target audience, and financial goals.

Remember, the adult content industry on OnlyFans presents unique opportunities and challenges. We will keep the primary focus on adult content throughout this chapter, providing you with tailored advice and strategies to navigate this niche effectively. So, let's dive in and unlock the secrets to monetizing your content and optimizing your earnings on OnlyFans

.

SETTING SUBSCRIPTION PRICES AND TIERS EFFECTIVELY

Setting the right subscription prices and designing tiered subscription models are crucial steps in monetizing your content effectively on OnlyFans. In this section, we will explore the key considerations and strategies to help you determine the most appropriate subscription prices and structure tiers that align with your target audience and maximize your earning potential.

Understand Your Value Proposition: Start by understanding your unique selling points, the quality of your content, and the value you provide to your subscribers. Consider factors such as the exclusivity of your content, your expertise, the level of personalization, and any additional perks or benefits you offer.

Research the Market: Conduct market research to gain insights into the pricing strategies of other creators in your niche. While it's important to differentiate yourself, analyzing the market can help you understand the general pricing trends and the expectations of your potential subscribers.

Consider Your Target Audience: Understand your target audience's spending habits, preferences, and expectations. Consider factors such as their demographics, disposable income, and the value they place on the type of content you provide. This will help you determine the price range that is reasonable and attractive to your target audience.

Test and Iterate: It's essential to continuously test and refine your pricing strategy based on feedback and performance. Experiment with different price points and tier structures to gauge subscriber response and adjust accordingly. Pay attention to metrics such as subscriber growth, retention rates, and feedback to optimize your pricing strategy over time.

Add Value with Different Tiers: Consider implementing tiered subscription models to offer different levels of access and benefits to your subscribers. Each tier can provide increasing value, such as exclusive content, personalized interactions, or special perks. This allows you to cater to different segments of your audience and provide options that align with their desired level of engagement.

Remember, finding the right balance between pricing and value is key. While you want to price your subscriptions competitively, ensure that the value you provide justifies the cost. Regularly assess and adjust your pricing strategy based on market trends, audience feedback, and the evolving nature of your content.

By employing these strategies and keeping your target audience's preferences and expectations in mind, you can set subscription prices and structure tiers effectively, maximizing your revenue potential while maintaining a loyal subscriber base.

EXPLORING ADDITIONAL REVENUE STREAMS

In addition to subscription fees, OnlyFans offers several other revenue streams that can further enhance your earnings and strengthen your connection with subscribers. In this section, we will explore various additional revenue streams and provide insights on how to effectively leverage them to maximize your monetization potential.

Tips: Encourage and incentivize your subscribers to tip you for your content. Tips are a great way for your fans to show appreciation for your work and can provide an additional source of income. Engage with your audience and offer exclusive perks or rewards to those who tip, creating a mutually beneficial relationship.

Pay-Per-View Content: Consider creating exclusive pay-per-view content that goes beyond your regular subscription offering. This can include special photosets, videos, or live streams that require an additional fee for access. Ensure that the content you provide justifies the price and offers a unique and compelling experience for your subscribers.

Custom Content Requests: Capitalize on the personal connections you've built with your subscribers by offering custom content requests. Allow them to request personalized photos, videos, or interactions for a fee. Tailor the content to their specific desires and preferences, making them feel valued and special. Set clear guidelines and boundaries for custom requests to ensure a positive and manageable experience for both you and your subscribers.

Merchandise Sales: Leverage your brand and fanbase by offering merchandise related to your content. This can include items such as t-shirts, posters, autographed photos, or even personal items used in your content (with appropriate legal considerations). Develop an online store or collaborate with platforms that facilitate merchandise sales to expand your revenue opportunities.

When exploring additional revenue streams, it's important to strike a balance between offering value to your subscribers and maintaining the integrity of your brand. Be transparent about the pricing and benefits associated with each revenue stream, and continually assess the response and feedback from your audience to optimize your offerings.

By exploring and effectively leveraging these additional revenue streams, you can diversify your income sources, deepen engagement with your subscribers, and enhance your overall monetization on OnlyFans.

COLLABORATIONS AND CROSS-PROMOTION OPPORTUNITIES

Collaborations and cross-promotion with other creators on OnlyFans can be a powerful strategy to expand your reach, attract new subscribers, and create mutually beneficial opportunities. In this section, we will explore the benefits of collaborations and share strategies for successfully engaging in cross-promotion with other creators.

1. BENEFITS OF COLLABORATIONS

Increased Exposure: Collaborating with other creators exposes you to their fanbase and vice versa, providing an opportunity to tap into new audiences who may be interested in your content.

Credibility and Trust: Partnering with established creators can enhance your credibility and trustworthiness among their fanbase, making it more likely for them to explore and subscribe to your content.

Variety and Diversity: Collaborations allow you to diversify your content and offer a fresh perspective to your subscribers. It can also introduce you to new content ideas and styles.

2. IDENTIFYING POTENTIAL PARTNERS

Target Audience Alignment: Look for creators whose target audience aligns with yours. Consider creators who produce complementary or related content to create a synergy that benefits both parties.

Engagement and Compatibility: Assess the engagement and compatibility of potential partners by reviewing their interactions with their fanbase, their content quality, and their communication style.

3. ESTABLISHING MUTUALLY BENEFICIAL ARRANGEMENTS

Clear Goals and Expectations: Communicate your goals and expectations to potential partners and ensure there is a mutual understanding of what each party aims to achieve from the collaboration.

Fair Exchange: Determine the value exchange for the collaboration. This could include sharing each other's content, promoting each other's profiles, or offering special discounts or perks to each other's subscribers.

Collaboration Formats: Explore different collaboration formats such as joint content creation, guest appearances on each other's platforms, or hosting joint events or giveaways. Be creative and find ways to provide unique experiences to both fanbases.

4. LEVERAGING EACH OTHER'S FANBASE:

Promotion and Shoutouts: Promote your collaboration through social media, OnlyFans messages, or on your respective profiles. Share sneak peeks, teasers, or behind-the-scenes content to generate excitement and anticipation.

Exclusive Offers: Consider offering exclusive perks or rewards to subscribers who engage with the collaboration. This could include discounted subscriptions, access to joint content, or special interactions.

Cross-Promotion Strategies: Collaborate on joint marketing efforts, such as sharing each other's content, featuring each other in your profile bios, or participating in joint promotional campaigns.

Remember to maintain open and clear communication with your collaboration partners throughout the process. Regularly evaluate the results and feedback from the collaboration to assess its impact on your reach, engagement, and monetization.

By strategically engaging in collaborations and cross-promotion, you can tap into new audiences, strengthen your presence on OnlyFans, and create exciting opportunities for both you and your collaboration partners.

SPONSORSHIPS AND BRAND PARTNERSHIPS

Sponsorships and brand partnerships present a valuable opportunity for creators on OnlyFans to generate additional income while collaborating with brands that align with their content and values. In this section, we will explore the process of pursuing sponsorships and brand partnerships, from identifying suitable brands to maintaining authenticity in sponsored content integration.

IDENTIFYING SUITABLE BRANDS
Alignment with Content: Look for brands whose products or services align with your content and target audience. Consider brands that

share similar values and complement the themes or topics you cover on OnlyFans.

Audience Relevance: Assess the relevance of the brand to your subscribers. Consider whether the brand's offerings would genuinely interest and benefit your audience.

Research and Outreach: Conduct research to identify potential brands that are active in your niche. Reach out to them through email or direct messages, expressing your interest in a potential collaboration.

NEGOTIATING AGREEMENTS

Define Deliverables: Clearly outline the scope of the collaboration and the deliverables expected from both parties. This may include sponsored posts, product reviews, promotional campaigns, or exclusive discounts for subscribers.

Compensation and Terms: Discuss the compensation structure and terms of the partnership, such as payment details, content usage rights, and exclusivity clauses. Negotiate a fair agreement that aligns with the value you bring to the brand.

Authenticity and Integration: Emphasize the importance of maintaining authenticity in sponsored content. Ensure that the brand's messaging integrates naturally into your content without compromising your unique style or voice.

MAINTAINING AUTHENTICITY IN SPONSORED CONTENT

Transparency and Disclosure: Clearly disclose sponsored content to your subscribers. Transparency builds trust and helps maintain authenticity in your relationship with your audience.

Genuine Recommendations: Ensure that you genuinely believe in the brand and its offerings. Only promote products or services that you have personally used and can genuinely recommend to your audience.

Creative Integration: Find creative ways to integrate sponsored content into your profile. Craft engaging and informative posts that provide value to your subscribers while showcasing the brand's products or services.

LONG-TERM PARTNERSHIPS:
Nurture Relationships: Focus on building long-term partnerships with brands by delivering quality sponsored content and maintaining open lines of communication. Strong relationships can lead to recurring collaborations and increased opportunities.

Track Results: Monitor and analyze the performance of sponsored content in terms of engagement, feedback from subscribers, and conversions. Use this data to refine your approach and demonstrate your value to potential future partners.

Remember, while pursuing sponsorships and brand partnerships can be lucrative, it is essential to select brands that align with your values and maintain authenticity in your content. By striking the right balance between monetization and maintaining a genuine connection with your audience, you can create mutually beneficial partnerships and generate additional income on OnlyFans.

AFFILIATE MARKETING STRATEGIES

Affiliate marketing is a powerful monetization strategy that allows creators on OnlyFans to earn commissions by promoting relevant products or services to their audience. In this section, we will explore the concept of affiliate marketing and provide guidance on how to leverage it effectively to generate revenue.

UNDERSTANDING AFFILIATE MARKETING

Commission-Based Model: Affiliate marketing involves promoting products or services through unique affiliate links. When a purchase is made through your affiliate link, you earn a commission.

Affiliate Networks: Explore affiliate networks and programs that are relevant to your niche and target audience. These networks connect creators with brands looking to partner with affiliates.

Disclosure: Transparently disclose affiliate links to your subscribers. Honesty and transparency help build trust and maintain authenticity with your audience.

SELECTING RELEVANT PRODUCTS OR SERVICES

Alignment with Your Niche: Choose products or services that align with your content and target audience. Consider the interests and preferences of your subscribers when selecting affiliate offers.

Quality and Reputation: Ensure that the products or services you promote are of high quality and have a positive reputation. Your recommendations should be genuine and beneficial to your audience.

IMPLEMENTING AFFILIATE LINKS

Affiliate Networks: Sign up for affiliate programs or networks that offer products or services relevant to your niche. These platforms provide unique affiliate links that track your referrals and commissions.

Placement: Strategically place affiliate links within your content, such as in blog posts, social media captions, or video descriptions. Ensure that the links are easily clickable and clearly labeled as affiliate links.

OPTIMIZING PROMOTIONAL EFFORTS

Contextual Integration: Integrate affiliate promotions seamlessly into your content by providing context and explaining how the product or service relates to your audience's needs or interests.

Value-Added Recommendations: Go beyond simply sharing the affiliate link. Provide valuable information, personal experiences, or reviews to help your audience make informed purchasing decisions.

Tracking and Analytics: Use tracking tools provided by the affiliate network to monitor the performance of your affiliate links. Analyze metrics such as clicks, conversions, and earnings to assess the effectiveness of your promotional efforts.

Familiarize yourself with OnlyFans' policies regarding affiliate marketing. Ensure that your promotional activities comply with the platform's guidelines to avoid any potential violations or penalties.

Affiliate marketing can be a lucrative revenue stream for creators on OnlyFans. By selecting relevant products or services, implementing affiliate links strategically, and optimizing your promotional efforts, you can generate additional income while providing value to your subscribers. Remember to maintain authenticity and prioritize the interests of your audience to build trust and credibility in your affiliate marketing endeavors.

PRICING STRATEGIES FOR CUSTOM CONTENT

When it comes to adult content on OnlyFans, offering custom content can be a highly lucrative and engaging way to cater to your subscribers' specific desires. In this section, we will delve into more in-depth pricing strategies for custom content to ensure that you set competitive and profitable prices while meeting the expectations of your audience.

ASSESSING TIME AND EFFORT

Start by assessing the time and effort required to produce custom content. Consider the various tasks involved, such as scripting, filming, editing, and any additional requests or specializations.

Calculate the average time it takes you to complete different types of custom content. This will help you determine a fair price that reflects the value of your time and expertise.

LEVEL OF CUSTOMIZATION

Establish different tiers of customization based on the level of personalization your subscribers desire. This can range from basic requests to highly specific and elaborate scenarios.

Price each tier accordingly, taking into account the additional time and effort required for more intricate customization. Consider offering a pricing menu that clearly outlines the options available at each tier.
Market Demand and Competition

Research the market demand for custom content in your niche. Look at what other creators are offering and how they price their custom content.

Take note of the pricing strategies used by successful creators who offer similar services. While you don't want to copy their prices exactly, it can provide valuable insights into the competitive landscape.

SUBSCRIBER FEEDBACK AND PREFERENCES

Regularly engage with your subscribers to understand their preferences and gather feedback on your custom content pricing. Consider conducting surveys or polls to gather insights.

Listen to your subscribers' opinions on your current pricing and any suggestions they may have. This feedback can help you refine your pricing structure and ensure it aligns with their expectations.

BUNDLED OFFERS AND DISCOUNTS

Consider offering bundled packages or discounted rates for subscribers who purchase multiple custom content requests or subscribe to higher tiers.

Bundling can create a sense of value for subscribers and incentivize them to invest more in your custom content offerings. Experiment with different bundle options and see which ones resonate the most with your audience.

ADJUSTMENTS AND FLEXIBILITY

Stay flexible with your pricing strategy. Periodically review and update your prices to reflect changes in market dynamics, subscriber preferences, and the value you provide.

Pay attention to trends and shifts in the market. If you notice a particular type of custom content becoming more or less popular, adjust your pricing accordingly to stay competitive.

Remember, pricing custom content requires a delicate balance between meeting the financial needs of your business and providing value to your subscribers. By assessing the time and effort involved, considering the level of customization, researching market demand, listening to your subscribers' feedback, and staying adaptable, you can set competitive prices that attract and retain customers while maximizing your earnings. Continuously monitor the effectiveness of your pricing strategy and make adjustments as needed to ensure long-term success on OnlyFans. Conclusion

In this chapter, we explored various monetization methods and pricing strategies specifically tailored for creators in the adult content industry on OnlyFans. Here are the key takeaways to remember as you embark on your monetization journey:

Setting Subscription Prices and Tiers: Carefully consider factors such as content quality, exclusivity, and perceived value when determining your subscription prices and structuring tiered subscription models. Strike a balance that attracts subscribers while ensuring your earnings reflect the value you provide.

Exploring Additional Revenue Streams: Leverage additional revenue streams like tips, pay-per-view content, custom content requests, and merchandise sales to diversify your income. Be strategic in implementing these options to engage subscribers and boost your earnings.

Collaborations and Cross-Promotion: Collaborating with other creators offers opportunities to expand your reach and attract new subscribers. Seek out mutually beneficial partnerships and leverage each other's fanbases to increase exposure and monetization prospects.

Sponsorships and Brand Partnerships: Integrating sponsored content can generate additional income. Prioritize authenticity and select brand partnerships that align with your values and resonate with your audience.

Affiliate Marketing Strategies: Explore affiliate marketing as a way to earn commissions. Choose relevant products or services, implement affiliate links effectively, and optimize your promotional efforts to generate revenue.

Pricing Strategies for Custom Content: Determine fair prices for custom content based on the time and effort involved, level of customization, market demand, and subscriber preferences. Offer bundled packages and discounts to incentivize subscribers to invest more in your custom content offerings.

It's important to remember that success on OnlyFans requires experimentation, ongoing evaluation, and adaptability. Continuously assess the effectiveness of your monetization methods and pricing strategies, and be open to making adjustments as needed. Stay connected with your audience, listen to their feedback, and always strive to provide value that keeps them engaged and satisfied.

As you apply the strategies discussed in this chapter, remember that finding the right monetization approach is a journey that evolves over time. Stay dedicated, stay connected, and stay creative. Your commitment to providing exceptional content and engaging with your subscribers will help you maximize your earning potential on OnlyFans.

Marketing & Promotion Techniques

Welcome to Chapter 7 of our comprehensive guide, where we explore the crucial marketing and promotion techniques that will propel your adult content to new heights on OnlyFans. In this chapter, we recognize the significance of employing effective strategies to not only attract new subscribers but also enhance your visibility within the platform's competitive landscape. By implementing targeted marketing efforts, you have the opportunity to showcase your unique adult content and connect with a wider audience. So, let's dive into the world of marketing and promotion on OnlyFans, and uncover the secrets to maximizing your growth and achieving unparalleled visibility in the adult content industry.

DEVELOPING A COMPELLING PERSONAL BRAND ON ONLYFANS

In order to stand out in the competitive world of adult content on On-lyFans, it's essential to develop a compelling personal brand that cap-tivates your target audience. Your personal brand is a reflection of your unique identity and what sets you apart from other creators. Here, we'll explore the key elements that contribute to a strong personal brand and provide practical tips to help you establish a memorable presence on OnlyFans.

Authenticity: Embrace your true self and let your authentic personality shine through in your content. Audiences are drawn to genuine creators who are unafraid to express themselves.

Uniqueness: Identify what makes you special and leverage it to differen-tiate yourself from the crowd. Whether it's a particular niche, a unique skill, or a captivating personality trait, emphasize these aspects to carve out your own niche on OnlyFans.

Consistent Messaging: Define your brand's core values and consistently communicate them through your content. This helps establish a sense of trust and reliability with your audience.

Choose a Memorable Username: Select a username that aligns with your personal brand and is easy to remember. It should reflect your con-tent, personality, or niche in a way that piques curiosity.

Craft an Engaging Bio: Your bio is your opportunity to make a strong first impression. Write a compelling and concise description that highlights your unique selling points and showcases what subscribers can expect from your content.

Design a Visually Appealing Profile: Pay attention to the visual aspects of your profile, including the profile picture and cover photo. Use high-quality images that represent your brand and captivate potential subscribers.

Remember, building a personal brand takes time and consistent effort. Continuously evaluate and refine your brand as you grow, ensuring that it remains true to your evolving identity as a creator. By developing a compelling personal brand, you'll attract the right audience and build a loyal fanbase on OnlyFans.

UNIQUE MARKETING STRATEGIES TO ATTRACT NEW SUBSCRIBERS

In a crowded market like OnlyFans, it's crucial to employ unique marketing strategies that captivate potential subscribers and set you apart from other creators. While traditional marketing methods have their place, thinking outside the box can help you attract a wider audience and drive more subscriptions. Here, we'll explore unconventional and creative marketing strategies that can help boost your visibility on OnlyFans.

Creating Teaser Content: Offer sneak peeks or teasers of your content to build intrigue and entice potential subscribers. This can be in the form of short video clips, captivating images, or engaging captions that leave your audience wanting more.

Storytelling in Promotional Materials: Incorporate storytelling techniques in your promotional materials to connect with your audience on a deeper level. Share personal anecdotes, experiences, or narratives that resonate with your target audience and create a sense of emotional connection.

Engaging Interactive Challenges or Games: Engage with potential subscribers by hosting interactive challenges or games that encourage participation. This could include contests, quizzes, or interactive polls that not only generate excitement but also provide valuable insights into your audience's preferences.

Leveraging User-Generated Content: Encourage your fans to create and share content related to your brand. This can include fan art, testimonials, or user-generated videos. Not only does this foster a sense of community, but it also serves as authentic social proof that can attract new subscribers.

PRACTICAL TIPS

Utilize Multiple Platforms: Promote your OnlyFans account across various platforms, such as social media, forums, or adult content communities. Adapt your marketing strategies to suit the specific platform and its audience.

Collaborate with Other Creators: Explore collaboration opportunities with other creators on OnlyFans. This can include joint promotions, shoutouts, or cross-promotions to tap into each other's fanbase and expand your reach.

Engage with Potential Subscribers: Actively interact with potential subscribers through comments, direct messages, or live sessions. Respond to their inquiries, show genuine interest, and build a personal connection to establish trust and rapport.

By implementing unique marketing strategies, you can create buzz, generate interest, and attract new subscribers to your OnlyFans account. Remember to adapt and experiment with different approaches to find what works best for your personal brand and target audience.

BUILDING A ONLINE PRESENCE THROUGH SOCIAL MEDIA MARKETING

In today's digital landscape, social media platforms play a crucial role in building a strong online presence and driving traffic to your OnlyFans profile. By leveraging these platforms effectively, you can expand your reach, engage with your target audience, and ultimately attract more subscribers. Additionally, content marketing techniques can further enhance your online presence and establish you as an authority in your niche. Here's how you can make the most of social media and content marketing to promote your OnlyFans account.

Choose the Right Social Media Platforms: Identify the social media platforms that align with your target audience and are conducive to promoting adult content. Platforms like Twitter, Instagram, Reddit, or even dating apps like Tinder can be valuable tools for reaching potential subscribers. Research the platform's policies regarding adult content and ensure you comply with their guidelines.

Craft Engaging Content: Develop valuable content that resonates with your target audience and showcases your expertise. This could include blog posts, videos, podcasts, or infographics related to your niche. Share tips, insights, and engaging stories that provide value to your audience and establish you as a trusted source of information.

Distribute and Promote Your Content: Utilize social media platforms to distribute and promote your content effectively. Share snippets or teasers of your content, directing viewers to your OnlyFans profile for the full experience. Engage with your audience by responding to comments, initiating discussions, and encouraging them to share your content with their networks.

Build Relationships with Influencers: Collaborate with influencers or established creators in your niche to amplify your reach. Partnering with influencers can help you tap into their existing audience and gain credibility through their endorsement. Seek out influencers who align with your brand values and target audience to maximize the impact of your collaborations.

Engage and Interact: Actively engage with your audience on social media by responding to comments, messages, and mentions. Encourage dialogue, ask for feedback, and show genuine interest in your followers. Building personal connections and nurturing relationships with your audience can foster loyalty and attract new subscribers.

PRACTICAL TIPS:
Use compelling visuals: Invest in high-quality visuals, including enticing images and videos, to capture attention and make a lasting impression on your audience.

Utilize hashtags: Research relevant and popular hashtags in your niche to increase the discoverability of your content and reach a wider audience.

By leveraging social media platforms effectively and implementing content marketing techniques, you can build a strong online presence, engage with your target audience, and drive traffic to your OnlyFans profile. Remember to consistently create valuable content, actively in-

teract with your audience, and adapt your strategies based on platform policies and audience preferences.
Collaborating with Fellow Creators

Engaging with the OnlyFans community and collaborating with fellow creators can be immensely valuable in expanding your reach, building relationships, and mutually benefiting from shared audiences. By actively participating in the community and fostering connections with other creators, you can amplify your visibility and attract more subscribers. Here are some practical tips on engaging with the OnlyFans community and collaborating with fellow creators:

Participate in Discussions: Join relevant forums, groups, or communities where creators and subscribers discuss topics related to adult content and OnlyFans. Contribute to conversations, share your insights, and offer support or advice to fellow creators. This not only helps you establish yourself as an engaged member of the community but also exposes you to potential subscribers who may be interested in your content.

Collaborate on Shoutouts or Promotions: Reach out to fellow creators who share a similar target audience and propose collaborations or shoutouts. This can involve featuring each other's profiles, sharing content, or even hosting joint events or promotions. Collaborations can help you tap into each other's fanbase and attract new subscribers who may be interested in your unique offerings.

Offer Exclusive Content Exchanges: Consider exchanging exclusive content with fellow creators to provide added value to your subscribers. This can involve featuring each other in videos, photo shoots, or custom content. By diversifying your content offerings and showcasing collaborations, you can attract new subscribers who are drawn to the unique experiences and variety you provide.

Attend Creator Events or Conferences: Look out for creator events or conferences related to adult content or online entrepreneurship. These gatherings provide opportunities to network with fellow creators, learn from industry experts, and discover potential collaboration opportunities. Networking in person can often lead to more meaningful connections and open doors for future collaborations.

Share Tips and Resources: Be generous with your knowledge and share valuable tips, resources, or insights with fellow creators. This helps build goodwill within the community and positions you as a helpful and supportive figure. In return, you may receive valuable advice, feedback, or even collaboration invitations from other creators.

Be authentic and genuine in your interactions with the OnlyFans community and fellow creators. Avoid being overly promotional or self-serving. Instead, focus on building meaningful relationships based on shared interests and mutual support.

Use direct messaging and private chats to establish one-on-one connections with creators who align with your brand and target audience. Personalized communication can lead to more fruitful collaborations and long-term relationships.

Follow and engage with creators whose content and style resonate with you. Show support by liking, commenting, and sharing their content. This reciprocity can lead to increased visibility and potential collaborations.

By actively engaging with the OnlyFans community and collaborating with fellow creators, you can expand your reach, tap into new audiences, and foster meaningful relationships. Remember to approach collaborations with a mindset of mutual benefit and authenticity, and be open to exploring unique partnership opportunities that align with your brand and audience.

CONCLUSION

In this chapter, we explored the essential marketing and promotion techniques that can help you maximize your success on OnlyFans. We discussed the importance of developing a compelling personal brand, leveraging unique marketing strategies, engaging with the OnlyFans community, and collaborating with fellow creators. Now, let's recap the key takeaways and encourage you to take action:

Build a Compelling Personal Brand: Your personal brand is what sets you apart from others. Focus on authenticity, uniqueness, and consistent messaging to attract and retain subscribers. Craft an engaging bio, choose a memorable username, and design a visually appealing profile that reflects your brand image.

Leverage Unique Marketing Strategies: Think outside the box when it comes to marketing. Create teaser content, incorporate storytelling into your promotions, engage potential subscribers through interactive challenges or games, and leverage user-generated content to attract a wider audience.

Establish a Strong Online Presence: Utilize social media platforms to build a strong online presence and drive traffic to your OnlyFans profile. Share valuable content related to your niche, such as blog posts, videos, or podcasts, and promote them effectively through social media channels.

Engage with the OnlyFans Community: Actively participate in discussions, join relevant groups or communities, and offer collaborations or shoutouts to fellow creators. By engaging with the community, you can expand your reach, build relationships, and tap into new subscriber pools.

Collaborate with Fellow Creators: Collaborating with fellow creators can lead to mutually beneficial opportunities. Seek out partnerships, exchange exclusive content, and attend creator events or conferences to network and discover potential collaborations.

Remember, marketing and promotion are ongoing processes. Continuously evaluate and refine your strategies based on audience feedback and market trends. Be open to experimentation, adapt to changes, and always strive to provide value to your subscribers.

Now it's time to take action! Implement the unique marketing techniques discussed in this chapter and monitor their effectiveness. Stay committed, be creative, and consistently promote your content to increase your visibility and attract new subscribers.

By leveraging effective marketing and promotion strategies, you can maximize your earning potential and achieve greater success on OnlyFans. Good luck on your journey, and remember that success comes to those who are willing to put in the effort and continuously evolve their approach.

Managing Your OnlyFans Business

Welcome to Chapter 8 of our guide, "Managing Your OnlyFans Business." In this chapter, we will delve into the crucial aspects of effectively managing your OnlyFans business to ensure its success and growth. While creating compelling content and engaging with your subscribers are vital, it's equally important to develop efficient strategies for time management, track your earnings and performance, and maintain professionalism in your customer interactions.

Managing an OnlyFans business requires a combination of organizational skills, financial acumen, and a customer-centric approach. By mastering the art of managing your business effectively, you can optimize your productivity, enhance customer satisfaction, and maximize your earning potential. This chapter will provide you with valuable insights and practical tips to help you navigate these critical aspects of your OnlyFans journey.

We will begin by exploring the importance of time management and setting boundaries. Running an OnlyFans business requires careful planning, prioritization, and establishing clear boundaries between your work and personal life. We will discuss practical strategies to help you allocate your time effectively, avoid burnout, and maintain a healthy work-life balance in the adult content industry.

Next, we will dive into the topic of tracking and analyzing your earnings and performance. Understanding your financial growth, subscriber engagement metrics, and revenue streams is vital for making informed decisions and identifying areas for improvement. We will introduce tools and techniques to track your earnings, analyze your performance, and optimize your business operations based on data-driven insights.

Customer service plays a crucial role in any business, including on OnlyFans. In the following section, we will discuss how to handle customer inquiries, requests, and maintain professionalism in your interactions. You'll learn effective communication strategies, timely response management, and how to handle special requests or custom content orders while maintaining appropriate boundaries with your subscribers.

Finally, we will address the importance of maintaining professionalism and protecting your privacy on OnlyFans. As an adult content creator, it's crucial to establish and uphold professional standards and safeguard your personal information. We will provide tips on maintaining a professional image, protecting your privacy, and setting clear guidelines for your interactions with subscribers.

By implementing the strategies and techniques discussed in this chapter, you will be equipped to effectively manage your OnlyFans business, achieve your goals, and nurture a thriving online presence. Let's dive in and discover the essential aspects of managing your OnlyFans business successfully!

TIME MANAGEMENT & SETTING BOUNDARIES

Running an OnlyFans business requires effective time management skills to ensure productivity, maintain a healthy work-life balance, and avoid burnout. In the adult content industry, where personal boundaries can easily blur, it's essential to establish clear guidelines and allocate your time wisely. Here are some practical tips to help you manage your time and set boundaries effectively:

Prioritize Tasks: Start by identifying your most important and time-sensitive tasks. Create a to-do list or use task management tools to stay organized and focused. Prioritize your content creation, engagement with subscribers, and essential administrative tasks.

Create a Schedule: Establish a structured schedule that aligns with your workflow and personal preferences. Set dedicated time slots for content creation, responding to messages, engaging with your audience, and managing administrative tasks. A consistent schedule will help you stay on track and maintain a sense of routine.

Set Boundaries: It's crucial to set boundaries between your work and personal life, even in the adult content industry. Define specific hours for work and make sure to take breaks and rest. Communicate your availability and response times to your subscribers, setting realistic expectations for engagement.

Delegate and Outsource: As your OnlyFans business grows, consider delegating or outsourcing certain tasks. Hiring a virtual assistant or collaborating with professionals for specific areas like graphic design or video editing can help alleviate your workload and allow you to focus on core aspects of your business.

Practice Self-Care: Taking care of yourself is paramount. Prioritize self-care activities, such as exercise, meditation, hobbies, and spending time with loved ones. Remember that your overall well-being directly impacts your creativity, productivity, and ability to provide quality content to your subscribers.

Learn to Say No: As tempting as it may be to accommodate every subscriber request, it's essential to set boundaries and learn to say no when necessary. Prioritize your own comfort level and artistic vision. It's crucial to maintain control over your content and avoid compromising your values or personal boundaries.

By implementing these time management strategies and setting clear boundaries, you'll be better equipped to manage your OnlyFans business effectively while maintaining a healthy work-life balance. Remember that finding the right balance is an ongoing process, so be open to adjusting your approach as your business evolves.

TRACKING & ANALYZING EARNINGS AND PERFORMANCE

Monitoring and analyzing your earnings and performance on OnlyFans is crucial for assessing the growth and success of your business. By understanding key metrics and trends, you can make informed decisions, identify areas for improvement, and optimize your revenue streams. Here are some steps to help you track and analyze your earnings and performance effectively:

Financial Tracking: Keep a detailed record of your earnings and expenses related to your OnlyFans business. This includes tracking subscription revenue, tips, pay-per-view sales, merchandise sales, and any other sources of income. Use accounting software or spreadsheets to maintain accurate financial records.

Performance Metrics: Evaluate your performance metrics to gain insights into subscriber engagement, content popularity, and audience demographics. Monitor metrics such as subscriber growth, post interactions (likes, comments, shares), views, and message response rates. OnlyFans provides built-in analytics tools, but you can also consider using third-party analytics platforms for more detailed insights.

Set Goals and Benchmarks: Establish goals and benchmarks to track your progress over time. This could include targets for subscriber growth, revenue milestones, or engagement metrics. Regularly assess your performance against these goals and adjust your strategies accordingly.

Identify Trends and Patterns: Analyze your data to identify trends and patterns in subscriber behavior and content performance. Look for correlations between certain types of content and higher engagement or revenue. This information can help you understand what resonates with your audience and guide your content creation strategy.

Experiment and Adapt: Use your data to inform your decision-making process. Experiment with different content formats, themes, or promotional strategies, and monitor the impact on your performance metrics. Adapt your approach based on what drives the best results for your business.

Continuous Learning: Stay informed about industry trends, marketing strategies, and platform updates. Attend webinars, read relevant articles, and engage with the OnlyFans community to stay ahead of the curve. The more you learn and apply new strategies, the better equipped you'll be to optimize your earnings and performance.

By diligently tracking and analyzing your earnings and performance metrics, you can gain a deeper understanding of your business's strengths and areas for improvement. This data-driven approach will help you make informed decisions, refine your content strategy, and maximize your earning potential on OnlyFans.

DEALING WITH CUSTOMER INQUIRIES AND RE-QUESTS

Providing exceptional customer service is crucial for building and maintaining a loyal subscriber base on OnlyFans. Effectively managing customer inquiries and requests requires professionalism, clear communication, and setting appropriate boundaries. Here are some strategies to help you navigate customer interactions:

Timely Response: Aim to respond to customer inquiries and messages in a timely manner. Set aside specific times during your work schedule to check and reply to messages, ensuring that subscribers feel valued and heard.

Clear Communication: Communicate with your subscribers in a clear and professional manner. Use proper grammar, be respectful, and address their concerns or questions directly. Avoid using offensive or derogatory language, as it can negatively impact your relationship with subscribers.

Setting Boundaries: Clearly define your boundaries and expectations with subscribers. Let them know what kind of content or requests you are willing to entertain and what is off-limits. Establishing these boundaries from the beginning helps manage expectations and avoid potential conflicts.

Handling Special Requests: Be open to considering special requests or custom content orders from your subscribers. Evaluate each request based on your comfort level and alignment with your brand. Clearly communicate any additional charges or terms associated with fulfilling these requests.

Professionalism: Maintain professionalism in all your interactions, regardless of the nature of the conversation. Treat each subscriber with respect and address their concerns or feedback in a professional manner. Avoid engaging in personal or inappropriate conversations.

Privacy and Consent: Respect your subscribers' privacy and obtain their consent before sharing or using any personal information they provide. Ensure that you adhere to OnlyFans' policies regarding data privacy and protection.

Escalation and Resolution: In the event of conflicts or issues with subscribers, have a protocol in place for escalation and resolution. If a situation becomes difficult to handle, consider reaching out to OnlyFans' support team for assistance and guidance.

Remember, exceptional customer service is key to building trust and fostering loyalty among your subscribers. By maintaining professionalism, setting boundaries, and addressing customer inquiries and requests in a timely and respectful manner, you can create a positive and engaging experience for your fans.

MAINTAINING PROFESSIONALISM & PROTECTING PRIVACY

Maintaining professionalism and protecting privacy are essential aspects of running a successful OnlyFans business in the adult content industry. Here are some tips to help you maintain professionalism and safeguard privacy:

Safeguard Personal Information: Protect your personal information by being cautious about what you share online. Avoid revealing sensitive details such as your real name, address, or contact information. Consider using a separate email address and phone number for your OnlyFans business to keep your personal and professional lives separate.

Set Privacy Preferences: Take advantage of the privacy settings and preferences available on the OnlyFans platform. Familiarize yourself with the platform's features and options for controlling who can access your content, view your profile, and interact with you. Adjust these settings based on your comfort level and desired level of privacy.

Establish Clear Guidelines: Set clear guidelines and expectations for interactions with subscribers. Clearly communicate what is acceptable and what is not in terms of language, behavior, and content requests. By establishing these boundaries, you can maintain control over your content and ensure a professional environment for both you and your subscribers.

Professional Image and Branding: Develop a professional image and branding that aligns with your desired reputation in the industry. Consider creating a consistent visual identity, including a professional profile picture, banner, and bio. Consistency in your branding helps establish trust and credibility among your subscribers.

Responding to Feedback and Reviews: Take feedback and reviews from your subscribers seriously. Respond to constructive criticism in a professional and respectful manner, demonstrating your commitment to providing a quality experience. Address any concerns raised by subscribers promptly and professionally.

Conflict Resolution: In the event of conflicts or disagreements with subscribers, handle the situation calmly and professionally. Avoid engaging in public arguments or disputes that could harm your reputation. If necessary, consider seeking mediation or involving OnlyFans' support team to help resolve the issue.

Protecting Content Ownership: Take measures to protect the ownership of your content. Familiarize yourself with copyright laws and consider watermarking your content or using digital rights management tools to prevent unauthorized use or distribution.

Remember, maintaining professionalism and protecting privacy are crucial for establishing a reputable and successful OnlyFans business. By safeguarding personal information, setting clear guidelines, and projecting a professional image, you can build trust and maintain a positive reputation within the adult content industry.

CONCLUSION

In this chapter, we delved into the crucial aspects of managing your OnlyFans business effectively. Here are the key takeaways:

Time management and setting boundaries: Efficiently managing your time and establishing clear boundaries between work and personal life are vital for maintaining a healthy work-life balance in the adult content industry. Prioritize tasks, create a schedule, and be mindful of the time you dedicate to your OnlyFans business.

Tracking and analyzing earnings and performance: Keep a close eye on your subscriber growth, engagement metrics, and revenue streams. By tracking and analyzing this data, you can identify areas for improvement, optimize your strategies, and maximize your earnings potential on OnlyFans.

Customer inquiries and requests: Providing excellent customer service is essential. Respond to inquiries in a timely manner, handle special requests professionally, and communicate clearly with your subscribers. Setting boundaries and maintaining professionalism will help establish a positive and respectful relationship with your audience.

Maintaining professionalism and protecting privacy: Protecting your personal information, setting privacy preferences, and establishing clear guidelines for interactions with subscribers are crucial for maintaining professionalism and safeguarding your privacy. Develop a professional image, respond to feedback and reviews professionally, and handle conflicts with professionalism.

By applying these strategies, you can effectively manage your OnlyFans business and increase your chances of long-term success. Remember to continually evaluate and adapt your business management practices to align with your evolving needs and goals.

Legal Considerations & Privacy Protection

In this chapter, we will delve into the crucial aspects of legal considerations and privacy protection when operating an adult content business on OnlyFans. As an OnlyFans creator, it is vital to have a clear understanding of the platform's policies, guidelines, and terms of service. Additionally, safeguarding your personal information and navigating potential legal issues are paramount to ensuring a safe and compliant business environment.

By familiarizing yourself with the policies and guidelines set forth by OnlyFans, you can ensure that your content and interactions align with the platform's standards. This knowledge will help you avoid any potential violations that could result in penalties or the suspension of your account. Understanding the rules and expectations set by OnlyFans allows you to maintain a professional presence while providing adult content to your subscribers.

Furthermore, protecting your privacy and personal information is of utmost importance in the adult content industry. We will discuss practical strategies and recommendations for safeguarding your personal data on OnlyFans, including managing your account privacy settings and adhering to best practices to mitigate privacy risks. Respecting the privacy of your subscribers is also crucial, as it establishes trust and fosters positive relationships.

Legal considerations, such as copyright and intellectual property rights, are significant aspects of running an OnlyFans business. We will explore the essentials of copyright laws, fair use, and how to protect your own content while respecting the intellectual property of others. Understanding these concepts will help you navigate potential infringements and safeguard your creative works.

It's essential to keep in mind that legal requirements and regulations can vary across jurisdictions. While we provide general guidance, it is advisable to consult with legal professionals who specialize in the adult content industry to ensure compliance with the laws applicable to your specific region.

By immersing yourself in the topics covered in this chapter and proactively addressing legal considerations and privacy protection, you can create a secure and thriving OnlyFans business. Let's dive into the various sections that will equip you with the knowledge and tools necessary to navigate the legal landscape and safeguard your privacy on the platform.

UNDERSTANDING ONLYFANS' POLICIES, GUIDELINES, & TERMS OF SERVICE

To successfully operate an adult content business on OnlyFans, it is crucial to have a comprehensive understanding of the platform's policies, guidelines, and terms of service. By familiarizing yourself with these key documents, you can ensure that your content and interactions align with the platform's standards, mitigate risks, and maintain a compliant presence on OnlyFans.

OnlyFans' policies and guidelines outline the acceptable and prohibited content, behavior, and activities on the platform. These policies help maintain a safe and respectful environment for creators and subscribers alike. By adhering to these guidelines, you can build a positive reputation and minimize the risk of account suspension or other penalties.

The terms of service govern the contractual relationship between creators and OnlyFans. It is essential to review and understand these terms to have a clear understanding of the platform's expectations, revenue-sharing models, and any rights and responsibilities that come with being an OnlyFans creator.

Key elements of OnlyFans' policies, guidelines, and terms of service may include:

Content Restrictions: Familiarize yourself with the types of content that are prohibited on OnlyFans, such as illegal content, non-consensual content, or content involving minors. Understanding and complying with these restrictions is essential for maintaining a lawful and ethical presence on the platform.

Copyright and Intellectual Property: Review OnlyFans' policies regarding copyright infringement and intellectual property rights. Respect the rights of others and ensure that your content does not infringe upon the intellectual property of others. Take appropriate measures to protect your own original content.

Prohibited Activities: Understand the activities that are not allowed on OnlyFans, such as spamming, harassment, or engaging in illegal or fraudulent practices. Adhering to these guidelines helps foster a professional and respectful community.

Age Verification: Comply with OnlyFans' age verification requirements to ensure that your content is accessible only to individuals of legal age. Age verification is a critical aspect of maintaining a compliant and responsible adult content business.

By taking the time to understand and adhere to OnlyFans' policies, guidelines, and terms of service, you demonstrate your commitment to operating within the platform's framework and provide a safe and reliable experience for your subscribers. Regularly reviewing these documents is essential, as they may be updated or modified by OnlyFans to align with evolving industry standards and legal requirements.

Remember, while we provide an overview of OnlyFans' policies in this section, it is advisable to refer to the official documentation provided by OnlyFans for the most up-to-date and accurate information. Additionally, consulting with legal professionals who specialize in the adult content industry can provide further clarity and guidance on navigating the platform's policies effectively.

PROTECTING YOUR PRIVACY ON ONLYFANS

As an adult content creator on OnlyFans, safeguarding your privacy and personal information is of paramount importance. By taking proactive measures to protect your privacy, you can create a secure environment for yourself and maintain trust with your subscribers. Here are some practical tips to help you protect your privacy on OnlyFans:

Manage Account Privacy Settings: Familiarize yourself with OnlyFans' privacy settings and customize them according to your preferences. Consider options such as restricting access to certain content or limiting visibility of your profile to specific regions or subscribers. Adjusting these settings can provide you with greater control over who can view and interact with your content.

Use Strong and Unique Passwords: Choose strong and unique passwords for your OnlyFans account, and consider using a password manager to securely store and manage your login credentials. Regularly update your passwords and avoid reusing them across multiple platforms to minimize the risk of unauthorized access.

Enable Two-Factor Authentication (2FA): Enable 2FA for your Only-Fans account to add an extra layer of security. With 2FA, you will need to provide a verification code in addition to your password when logging in, making it significantly more challenging for unauthorized individuals to access your account.

Be Mindful of Personal Information: Exercise caution when sharing personal information on OnlyFans. Only provide information that is necessary for your business operations and avoid sharing sensitive details such as your real name, address, or contact information publicly. Consider using a separate email address and pseudonym to maintain anonymity if desired.

Consent and Boundaries: Respecting subscribers' privacy rights is essential. Seek explicit consent before sharing any personal information, photos, or videos that may reveal your identity. Be mindful of boundaries and avoid crossing any lines that may compromise your privacy or the privacy of others.

Educate Yourself on Privacy Best Practices: Stay informed about privacy best practices and evolving privacy concerns in the adult content industry. Regularly educate yourself on topics such as data protection, online security, and privacy regulations to ensure that you are implementing the latest strategies to protect your privacy.

Be Prepared for Potential Risks: Despite your best efforts, there is always a possibility of privacy breaches or risks. Develop a plan for handling potential privacy incidents, such as unauthorized sharing of content or personal information. Familiarize yourself with OnlyFans' reporting mechanisms and procedures for addressing privacy concerns.

By implementing these privacy protection measures, you can minimize the risk of privacy breaches and maintain a secure environment for your OnlyFans business. Remember, maintaining privacy is an ongoing process, and it requires diligence and regular evaluation of your privacy practices to adapt to evolving threats and privacy concerns.

Note: While we provide general privacy protection tips in this section, it is advisable to consult with legal professionals or privacy experts to ensure that you are implementing the most appropriate privacy measures for your specific circumstances.

Copyright & Intellectual Property Rights

When operating an adult content business on OnlyFans, it is crucial to understand and navigate the legal considerations surrounding copyright and intellectual property rights. By familiarizing yourself with these concepts, you can protect your own content and ensure that you respect the intellectual property of others. Here are some key points to consider:

Copyright Basics: Copyright is a legal right that grants creators exclusive control over the use and distribution of their original works. Understand that your content, including photos, videos, and written material, is automatically protected by copyright as soon as it is created. It is essential to respect the copyright of others and to protect your own work from unauthorized use.

Fair Use: Familiarize yourself with the concept of fair use, which allows limited use of copyrighted material without permission from the copyright owner for specific purposes such as criticism, commentary, or educational purposes. However, the boundaries of fair use can be complex, and it is advisable to seek legal guidance if you are unsure whether your use of copyrighted material falls within fair use.

Respecting Intellectual Property: It is important to respect the intellectual property rights of others. Avoid using or distributing copyrighted material without obtaining the necessary permissions or licenses. This includes using copyrighted music, images, or videos in your content without proper authorization. Consider using royalty-free music and images or obtaining licenses for any copyrighted material you wish to incorporate into your content.

Protecting Your Content: Take steps to protect your own content from unauthorized use. Consider adding watermarks, logos, or copyright notices to your photos and videos to clearly establish your ownership. Additionally, you can include copyright statements in your profile or content descriptions to notify others that your work is protected.

Dealing with Copyright Infringements: If you encounter instances where your content is being used without your permission, take appropriate action. Start by documenting the infringement, including screenshots or other evidence. Then, reach out to the individual or platform using your content without authorization, requesting that they remove it immediately. If necessary, you may need to escalate the matter by filing a copyright infringement notice with the platform or seeking legal advice.

Seeking Legal Guidance: Copyright and intellectual property laws can be complex, and it is advisable to consult with legal professionals who specialize in intellectual property to ensure that you fully understand your rights and obligations. They can provide guidance on protecting your own content, responding to infringements, and navigating the legal landscape surrounding copyright and intellectual property.

Remember, respecting copyright and intellectual property is not only legally required but also contributes to a fair and ethical online environment. By understanding these legal considerations and taking proactive steps to protect your own content, you can operate your OnlyFans business with integrity while safeguarding the creative works of others. Compliance with Applicable Laws & Regulations

Compliance with applicable laws and regulations is paramount when operating an adult content business on OnlyFans. As the adult industry is subject to specific legal challenges, it is essential to understand and adhere to the relevant laws and regulations. Here are some key points to consider:

Age Verification Requirements: One of the crucial aspects of compliance in the adult content industry is ensuring that all participants, including creators and subscribers, are of legal age. Familiarize yourself with the age verification requirements in your jurisdiction and implement reliable methods to verify the age of your subscribers. OnlyFans provides built-in age verification mechanisms, but it is important to understand and comply with any additional legal requirements specific to your location.

Content Restrictions: Different jurisdictions may have specific regulations regarding the type of content that can be shared on adult platforms. It is essential to familiarize yourself with these restrictions and ensure that your content aligns with the legal guidelines. Examples of regulated content may include explicit sexual acts, violence, or activities involving minors. By understanding and complying with content restrictions, you can mitigate legal risks and maintain a responsible approach to your business.

Obscenity Laws: Obscenity laws vary from jurisdiction to jurisdiction, and it is crucial to understand the legal standards in your operating area. While OnlyFans provides a platform for adult content, it is important to ensure that your content does not cross the boundaries of obscenity as defined by the law. Familiarize yourself with the criteria for obscenity in your jurisdiction, such as the Miller test in the United States, and ensure that your content remains within legal boundaries.

Staying Informed and Seeking Professional Advice: The legal landscape surrounding the adult content industry is dynamic and subject to change. It is important to stay informed about legal developments, including new regulations, court decisions, or industry guidelines that may impact your business. Regularly review the terms of service and policies of OnlyFans to stay updated on platform-specific requirements. Additionally, consider seeking professional advice from attorneys specializing in adult entertainment law to ensure compliance with applicable laws and regulations.

Records Keeping: Some jurisdictions require adult content creators to maintain proper records of age verification, model releases, and other documentation. Understand the records-keeping obligations in your jurisdiction and implement appropriate systems to maintain and securely store these records.

Remember, compliance with laws and regulations not only helps protect your business but also contributes to the overall reputation and legitimacy of the adult content industry. By staying informed, seeking professional advice when necessary, and actively ensuring compliance, you can operate your OnlyFans business responsibly and confidently.

Maximizing Success & Future Trends

Welcome to Chapter 10 of our guide, where we delve into the crucial aspects of maximizing your success on OnlyFans and navigating future trends in the adult content industry. As an OnlyFans creator, you understand the dynamic nature of this platform and the need to continuously evolve and adapt to stay ahead of the curve.

In this chapter, we will explore strategies for building a solid foundation for long-term success, adapting to industry trends and market changes, and exploring potential opportunities beyond OnlyFans. Our aim is to equip you with the knowledge and insights necessary to thrive in this competitive landscape.

Maximizing your success on OnlyFans goes beyond simply posting content. It requires a strategic approach, continuous improvement, and a deep understanding of your audience's needs and desires. By adopting the right strategies, staying informed about industry trends, and embracing new opportunities, you can unlock your full earning potential and establish a lasting presence in the adult content market.

Furthermore, we will explore how you can forge professional relationships, collaborate with other creators, and embrace technological advancements to elevate your content and engage your audience in innovative ways. By nurturing these connections and staying open to new ideas, you can expand your reach, attract new subscribers, and create mutually beneficial opportunities.

However, it's important to remember that the adult content industry operates within its own unique legal framework. As you explore the strategies outlined in this chapter, always ensure compliance with the laws and regulations of your jurisdiction. Seek legal advice when necessary to protect yourself, your content, and your business.

Now, let's dive into the strategies and insights that will help you maximize your success on OnlyFans and navigate the ever-evolving landscape of the adult content industry. Get ready to unlock your full potential and position yourself for long-term growth and prosperity.

BUILDING A FOUNDATION FOR LONG-TERM SUCCESS

To achieve long-term success on OnlyFans, it's essential to build a solid foundation that fosters loyalty, consistency, and continuous improvement. In this section, we will explore strategies to help you establish a strong footing and cultivate a thriving community of loyal fans.

Cultivating a Loyal Fan Base Building a loyal fan base is crucial for sustained success on OnlyFans. Focus on engaging with your subscribers, making them feel valued, and creating a sense of exclusivity. Consider these strategies:

Interact with your fans regularly by responding to messages, comments, and requests.

Offer personalized experiences, such as custom content or shoutouts, to make subscribers feel special.

Foster a sense of community by encouraging interaction between fans and creating a supportive environment.

Maintaining a Consistent Posting Schedule Consistency is key to keeping your subscribers engaged and coming back for more. Develop a posting schedule that suits your availability and stick to it. Consider these tips:

Plan your content in advance to ensur: a steady stream of updates.

Use scheduling tools to automate posts and maintain a consistent presence.

Experiment with different types of content (photos, videos, live streams) to keep your feed diverse and engaging.

Continuous Improvement of Content Regularly improving the quality of your content is essential for attracting and retaining subscribers. Take the following steps to enhance your offering:

Seek feedback from your audience and adapt your content based on their preferences.

Invest in high-quality equipment, such as cameras and lighting, to improve the visual appeal of your content.

Experiment with different themes, styles, or niches to cater to a wider audience and keep your content fresh.

Nurturing Subscriber Relationships Developing strong relationships with your subscribers is crucial for long-term success. Engage with your audience and make them feel connected to you. Consider these approaches:

Offer behind-the-scenes glimpses into your life or creative process.
Run exclusive promotions or giveaways for your loyal subscribers.
Show genuine interest in your subscribers' lives and actively engage with their content.

By focusing on building a solid foundation for your OnlyFans business, you can cultivate a loyal fan base, maintain a consistent presence, continuously improve your content, and nurture strong subscriber relationships. These elements will form the cornerstone of your long-term success on the platform.

ADAPTING TO INDUSTRY TRENDS & MARKET CHANGES

In the fast-paced world of the adult content market, it's crucial to stay ahead of industry trends and adapt your strategies to meet evolving consumer preferences. This section will explore the importance of staying current and provide guidance on how to adapt your content, marketing strategies, and overall approach to align with industry trends.

Understanding Emerging Trends Stay informed about emerging trends in the adult content market to remain relevant and appealing to your audience. Consider the following sources for insights:

Follow industry news and publications to stay updated on the latest trends and developments.

Engage with your peers and fellow creators to exchange ideas and learn from each other's experiences.

Monitor social media platforms and online communities related to adult content to gauge emerging interests and preferences.

Embracing Technological Advancements Technology plays a significant role in shaping the adult content market. Embrace technological advancements to enhance your content and reach a wider audience. Consider the following strategies:

Explore new platforms or features that cater to the adult content market, such as live streaming or virtual reality experiences.

Experiment with innovative production techniques, such as interactive content or immersive storytelling.

Leverage data analytics tools to gain insights into your audience's behavior and preferences.

Responding to Shifts in Consumer Preferences Consumer preferences and desires can change over time. It's essential to stay attuned to these shifts and adapt your content and marketing strategies accordingly. Consider the following approaches:

Conduct regular surveys or polls to gather feedback and understand your audience's evolving preferences.

Experiment with different content styles, genres, or themes to cater to diverse interests.

Keep a close eye on audience engagement metrics to identify trends and patterns that resonate with your subscribers.

Flexibility & Experimentation Maintaining a spirit of flexibility and experimentation is crucial when adapting to industry trends and market changes. Embrace a mindset of continuous improvement and be willing to try new approaches. Consider the following suggestions:

Test new content formats, promotional strategies, or collaborations to gauge their effectiveness.

Seek feedback from your audience and use it as a guide for making informed adjustments to your content and marketing efforts.

Monitor the performance of your content and campaigns, and be open to refining or pivoting your strategies based on the results.

By staying current with industry trends, embracing technological advancements, responding to shifts in consumer preferences, and fostering a spirit of flexibility and experimentation, you can adapt your content, marketing strategies, and overall approach to thrive in the ever-changing adult content market.

EXPLORING OPPORTUNITIES BEYOND ONLY-FANS

While OnlyFans provides a robust platform for monetizing your adult content, it's important to explore opportunities beyond its boundaries to maximize your growth potential. This section will discuss the benefits of diversifying your income streams and exploring new avenues for expansion.

Launching a Personal Website Consider launching your own personal website to establish a more comprehensive online presence. A personal website offers several advantages:

Greater control over your brand image and content distribution.

Ability to offer additional features and exclusive content to your subscribers.

Opportunity to monetize your website through subscriptions, ad placements, or premium content offerings.

Ensure that your website complies with relevant laws and regulations, and prioritize privacy and security measures to protect your subscribers' information.

Offering Additional Services Consider offering additional services that complement your adult content, providing added value to your subscribers. These services could include:

One-on-one video calls or live cam sessions for a more intimate and personalized experience.

Exclusive access to private events, parties, or meet-and-greet sessions. Consultation services for aspiring adult content creators or personalized advice on relationships and sexuality.

Advertise these services on your OnlyFans profile and leverage your existing subscriber base to generate interest and bookings.

Expanding Presence on Other Platforms and Collaborations Extend your reach by expanding your presence on other adult content platforms or collaborating with mainstream media outlets. This can provide exposure to new audiences and opportunities for growth:

Explore other adult content platforms that align with your brand and target audience.

Collaborate with mainstream media outlets, such as magazines or podcasts, to share your expertise and reach a wider audience.

Engage in cross-promotion with fellow creators to tap into each other's fan bases and increase visibility.

Be mindful of the terms and guidelines of each platform or collaboration to ensure they align with your personal brand and values.

By diversifying your income streams, exploring new avenues for growth, and expanding your presence beyond OnlyFans, you can maximize your success and create a sustainable business model that extends well beyond a single platform.

Professional Relationships & Collabo-rations

In the adult content industry, building strong professional relationships and engaging in collaborations can significantly enhance your success. This section focuses on the importance of networking, partnering with other creators, and engaging with industry influencers to foster growth and expand your reach.

Networking within the Adult Content Community Networking within the adult content community can open doors to valuable connections, knowledge sharing, and potential collaborations. Here are some tips to help you nurture professional relationships:

Engage in online communities and forums specific to the adult content industry. Participate in discussions, offer insights, and connect with like-minded creators.

Attend adult industry events, conferences, and trade shows to meet industry professionals, share experiences, and explore potential collaborations.

Utilize social media platforms to connect with other creators, engage with their content, and build mutually beneficial relationships.

Remember to approach networking with authenticity and respect, focusing on building genuine connections rather than just seeking immediate benefits.

Partnering with Other Creators Collaborating with other creators can be a powerful way to expand your audience and reach. Here's how you can approach collaborations effectively:

Identify creators whose content and values align with yours. Look for complementary niches or shared target audiences to ensure a mutually beneficial partnership.

Reach out to potential collaborators with a clear proposition and explain how both parties can benefit from the collaboration.

Explore various collaboration formats, such as creating joint content, featuring each other in your respective content, or offering special promotions to each other's subscribers.

By collaborating with other creators, you can tap into their fan base and introduce your content to new audiences, leading to increased exposure and potential subscriber growth.

Engaging with Industry Influencers Engaging with industry influencers can provide opportunities for mentorship, exposure, and valuable insights. Consider the following strategies:

Identify influencers in the adult content industry who have a strong presence and a loyal following. Engage with their content by commenting, sharing, and offering valuable contributions.

Attend events or webinars where influencers are speaking or participating, and take advantage of networking opportunities.

Reach out to influencers with personalized messages expressing your admiration for their work and expressing your interest in potential collaborations or partnerships.

Building relationships with influencers can help you gain visibility, establish credibility, and open doors to new opportunities in the industry.

Remember, nurturing professional relationships and engaging in collaborations require mutual respect, clear communication, and a focus on creating value for all parties involved. By fostering these relationships, you can create a supportive network within the adult content industry and unlock new avenues for growth and success.

TECHNOLOGY & INNOVATIVE STRATEGIES

Technology plays a significant role in shaping the adult content industry and providing new opportunities for creators to maximize their success. This section focuses on exploring the role of technology and discussing innovative strategies that can help you engage your audience and stand out from the competition.

Virtual Reality (VR) Experiences Virtual reality (VR) has revolutionized the way content is consumed and experienced. Consider the following when embracing VR technology:

Explore the potential of creating immersive VR experiences that allow your subscribers to engage with your content in a more interactive and immersive way.

Invest in VR equipment and tools to enhance the quality and realism of your VR content.

Collaborate with VR content creators or studios to produce high-quality VR experiences that cater to the preferences of your audience.

By incorporating VR experiences into your content, you can provide a unique and captivating experience for your subscribers, setting yourself apart from others in the industry.

Interactive Content Interactive content allows you to actively engage your audience and create a more personalized experience. Consider these strategies:

Experiment with interactive elements such as polls, quizzes, or choose-your-own-adventure style content to encourage active participation from your subscribers.

Offer interactive live streaming sessions where subscribers can interact with you in real-time through chat, comments, or interactive games.

Utilize interactive platforms or tools that enable subscribers to customize their experience or request specific content.

By incorporating interactive elements into your content, you can deepen the connection with your audience, increase engagement, and provide a more tailored experience.

Subscription Bundling Subscription bundling involves offering different tiers or packages that provide additional value to your subscribers. Consider the following strategies:

Create tiered subscription levels with varying access to exclusive content, personalized interactions, or additional perks.

Offer bundle packages that combine access to your OnlyFans content with other premium services, such as merchandise, personalized videos, or private chat sessions.

Provide loyalty rewards or discounts for subscribers who commit to longer subscription periods or upgrade to higher tiers.
Subscription bundling can incentivize subscribers to invest more in their relationship with you, leading to increased retention and revenue.

Remember, embracing technological advancements and exploring innovative strategies requires a willingness to adapt and experiment. Stay informed about the latest developments in the industry, seek feedback from your audience, and be open to incorporating new technologies and approaches to engage your subscribers effectively.

By leveraging technology and embracing innovation, you can create a unique and captivating experience for your audience, drive subscriber growth, and maximize your success in the adult content industry.

CONCLUSION

We have explored strategies for maximizing success and staying ahead in the ever-evolving world of adult content on OnlyFans. By implementing the discussed strategies, you can enhance your presence, engage your audience, and open doors to new opportunities. Let's recap the key takeaways:

Building a Foundation for Long-Term Success: Cultivate a loyal fan base, maintain consistency in your posting schedule, and continuously improve the quality of your content. Nurture subscriber relationships and leverage feedback to enhance your offering.

Adapting to Industry Trends and Market Changes: Stay current with industry trends, technological advancements, and shifts in consumer preferences. Adapt your content, marketing strategies, and overall approach to align with these trends and cater to your audience's evolving interests.

Exploring Opportunities Beyond OnlyFans: Diversify your income streams by exploring opportunities beyond OnlyFans. Consider launching a website, selling merchandise, or offering additional services to expand your revenue sources. Expand your presence on other platforms and collaborate with mainstream media outlets to broaden your reach.

Nurturing Professional Relationships and Collaborations: Foster professional relationships and collaborations within the adult content industry. Network with other creators, engage with industry influencers, and leverage each other's audiences for growth and exposure.

Embracing Technological Advancements and Innovative Strategies: Embrace technologies like virtual reality (VR) experiences, interactive content, and subscription bundling to provide unique and captivating experiences for your audience. Experiment with new technologies and innovative approaches to engage and retain your subscribers.

Remember, success on OnlyFans requires adaptability, continuous learning, and a commitment to staying ahead of industry trends. Be open to embracing new opportunities, technologies, and strategies that align with your brand and cater to your audience's desires. Stay informed, seek feedback, and be willing to experiment and evolve your approach.

By implementing these strategies and maintaining a proactive mindset, you can maximize your success on OnlyFans and position yourself for long-term growth in the adult content industry. Keep pushing boundaries, stay connected with your audience, and continually refine your approach to achieve your goals on OnlyFans.

RECAP

As we conclude this comprehensive guide on maximizing success on OnlyFans, it is essential to reflect on the valuable insights and strategies that have been shared. Throughout this journey, we have explored various aspects of running a successful OnlyFans business, from creating compelling content to effective monetization strategies, marketing and promotion techniques, managing the business, and navigating legal considerations. We sincerely hope that this guide has provided you with a solid foundation to thrive in the adult content industry.

Let us take a moment to recap the key points covered in each chapter. We began by discussing the importance of identifying your niche and target audience, emphasizing the need for authenticity and engaging content. We then delved into the intricacies of monetization, exploring subscription pricing, additional revenue streams, sponsorships, and affiliate marketing. Next, we focused on marketing and promotion techniques, highlighting the significance of developing a compelling personal brand, leveraging unique marketing strategies, engaging with the OnlyFans community, and collaborating with fellow creators.

Now, as you embark on your journey towards maximizing your success on OnlyFans, we want to offer our heartfelt encouragement and share some final thoughts. The adult content industry is a dynamic and ever-evolving landscape, presenting both opportunities and challenges. However, with the knowledge and insights gained from this guide, you are equipped to navigate these waters with confidence.

Remember, success on OnlyFans requires dedication, perseverance, and an unwavering commitment to delivering value to your subscribers. Stay true to yourself, embrace your uniqueness, and consistently strive to improve your craft. While challenges may arise along the way, view them as opportunities for growth and learning.

We also want to emphasize the importance of staying adaptable and responsive to industry trends. The adult content market is continuously evolving, and being aware of emerging trends and technologies can give you a competitive edge. Embrace new platforms, explore innovative strategies, and be open to experimenting with different approaches to engage and delight your audience.

As we bring this guide to a close, we want to express our deepest gratitude for accompanying us on this journey. We hope that the insights and strategies shared have provided you with a solid foundation to embark on a successful OnlyFans business. Remember, success is not guaranteed overnight, but with consistent effort, a passion for your craft, and a focus on providing value to your subscribers, you have the potential to achieve great heights.

Finally, we encourage you to take action. Apply the strategies discussed in this guide, adapt them to your unique style and niche, and consistently evaluate and refine your approach. Surround yourself with a supportive community of fellow creators, seek guidance when needed, and never stop learning and growing.

Wishing you the utmost success in your OnlyFans journey!

AFTER WORD

As we conclude our journey through "Building a Brand in Adult Content: OnlyFans Formula," it is my hope that this guide has not only equipped you with the tools and knowledge to thrive on OnlyFans, but also inspired you to embrace your creative journey with confidence and enthusiasm.

The landscape of digital content creation, particularly in the adult entertainment sector, is one that is constantly evolving. Platforms like OnlyFans have not only disrupted traditional models but have also opened up new avenues for creators to express themselves, connect with audiences, and build sustainable careers. In navigating this landscape, your resilience, adaptability, and commitment to your craft will be your greatest assets.

Remember, the path to success on OnlyFans, as in any creative endeavor, is unique to each individual. While this book has provided strategies, tips, and insights, the real magic lies in how you adapt these learnings to your personal brand, your content, and your community. Stay true to your voice, be consistent in your efforts, and always prioritize the well-being and respect of both yourself and your audience.

As you move forward, keep in mind the importance of community. OnlyFans is not just a platform; it's a global stage where creators and fans alike come together to share, celebrate, and support one another. Engaging with your audience, collaborating with fellow creators, and being an active member of this community can enrich your experience and open up even more opportunities for growth and success.

The journey of a content creator is filled with highs and lows, triumphs and challenges. There will be moments of doubt, but also moments of incredible fulfillment. Embrace each phase of your journey with an open heart and a willingness to learn. Every experience, every interaction, is a stepping stone towards achieving your goals.

As the digital world continues to evolve, so too will the opportunities and challenges you face. Stay informed, be flexible, and never stop exploring new ways to enhance your craft and your brand. Your journey on OnlyFans is not just about financial success; it's about expressing your creativity, connecting with others, and making a mark in a dynamic and ever-changing industry.

Lastly, I encourage you to view your venture on OnlyFans as more than a business; see it as a journey of self-discovery and personal growth. Each day offers a new opportunity to explore your potential, to connect with people from around the world, and to share a part of yourself in ways that only you can.

Thank you for allowing this guide to be a part of your OnlyFans journey. As you turn the final page, know that your adventure is just beginning. Here's to your success, your growth, and your vibrant future on OnlyFans. Go forth with passion, creativity, and confidence. The world is waiting to see what you will create.

About the Author

Mia Phoenix, stands as a distinguished expert and coach in the world of OnlyFans content creation. Her journey in this innovative digital landscape is marked by a passionate commitment to guiding and empowering women to carve out their independent paths. With a deep understanding of the platform's nuances, Mia has become a pivotal figure in helping numerous creators overcome challenges and harness their unique strengths for success.

Her mission transcends the boundaries of mere coaching; Mia is dedicated to empowering women to take control of their digital presence and financial futures. She believes fervently in the transformative potential of OnlyFans as a tool for self-expression, community building, and economic independence. Through her guidance and expertise, Mia Phoenix has become a beacon of inspiration and support, paving the way for a new generation of confident, independent digital content creators.

BOOKS BY AUTHOR

MASTERING CONSUMER PSYCHOLOGY: ONLYFANS FORMULA

"Ever wonder what really drives your customers' decisions?"

Dive into the world of consumer psychology with " Mastering Consumer Psychology: OnlyFans Formula". This book is your ultimate guide to understanding what drives your audience's decisions and how to appeal to their deepest motivations. With a focus on the OnlyFans platform, this insightful guide reveals the psychological underpinnings that can make or break your success in the adult content industry.

Inside, you'll find:
- The role of psychological triggers in consumer decision-making.
- Understanding consumer motivations and needs.
- Techniques for crafting persuasive and influential messages.
- Using consumer segmentation for targeted marketing.
- Exploring the dynamics of online addiction.
- The impact of social media on consumer psychology.
- The influence of cultural factors on consumer psychology.
- Insights into the adult content industry and consumer behavior.

"Mastering Consumer Psychology: OnlyFans Formula:" is more than just a guide; it's the key to unlocking a deeper connection with your audience, enhancing your content's appeal, and boosting your success on OnlyFans.

Transform your approach, captivate your audience, and achieve unparalleled success by applying the principles of consumer psychology today.

Books by Author

Creative Sparks For Quality Content: OnlyFans Formula
Finding it hard to stand out on OnlyFans?

Break through the noise on OnlyFans. "Creative Sparks For Quality Content" is filled with fresh ideas and creative approaches to ensure your content grabs attention and keeps it. Discover how to make every OnlyFans post count. Learn from industry experts how to create distinct, engaging content that captures the essence of your unique style.

Inside, you'll find:
- Craft uniquely memorable content that truly sets you Apart.
- Align your creative passions directly with audience interests.
- Precisely match your content with your audience's needs & wants.
- Effortlessly overcome creative blocks for consistent content flow.
- Zero in on and dominate your ideal niche.
- Distinguish yourself boldly in a highly competitive niche.
- Master the art of strategic content planning and scheduling.
- Expertly manage & respond to your fans' feedback.

Envision your OnlyFans profile standing out, attracting new subscribers effortlessly, and retaining them with compelling content. Look forward to effortlessly overcoming the challenges of content creation, becoming a leading voice and trendsetter in your niche.

Begin creating content that captivates – your journey starts with this book.